What Is a Campus Magazine?

The publication you hold in your hands is really a book in magazine format. Books generally have more in-depth content, but let's face it, we'd all rather read a magazine. Most of us are so used to being entertained that we can hardly stand to pick up a real live book and read it through.

Because of this, we have designed these Campus Magazines to be a little crazy. We've filled them with quizzes, spoof ads, jokes, trivia, photos, cartoons, Bible studies, and interesting but short articles.

(Just in case someone misses the point of the spoof advertisements in this Campus Magazine, may I point out that they are for products that don't exist. Any similarity to any product already in existence is purely coincidental.)

If you enjoy Romance, you might want to pick up some of the other Campus Magazines (especially Date, Date II, Love, Communicate, and Marry.) You will find a list of the additional titles available in this series on the back cover. May God bless you!

Romance

romance ro′-mans, [ME *romauns,*

romaunce, fr. OF *romans, romanz*] French

4 a : (1) a love, love affair, or marriage

of a romantic nature (2) Lovemaking

b : an attraction or aspiration of an

emotional or romantic character.

It Must Be Love

*L*arissa Childs tried not to absorb the aroma of Rod Johnston's after-shave lotion as he walked by. But as she breathed in that smell a shiver traveled up her spine. Just knowing Rod was going to walk up the aisle, past her seat, toward the front of Mr. Clausen's math class, was enough to put her senses in a spin.

As Rod passed, Larissa's gaze sheepishly followed the tall football player. *Why do you affect me like this?* she silently asked. *What makes you so special? Why am I so crazy about you?*

It wasn't that Rod was the best-looking guy in class, or even the most popular; in fact, Larissa considered her popularity and circle of friends to be much more socially acceptable than his. What was it then? Was it the smile

that covered his entire face?

In every other area of her life, Larissa was in total control. She prided herself on having a clean room, good grades, and a fashionable and attractive appearance. She knew who she was and where she was going. That's why these strong feelings for Rod Johnston were so unnerving. She didn't like the fact that someone could have such a big impact upon her feelings—and not even know it.

Yes, she said to herself, as Rod picked up his algebra paper and returned to his desk, *you'll never know how you affected me. I refuse to let you. . . .* Then his fragrant after-shave reached her again and she felt that same uncontrollable sinking feeling deep within.

What causes those involuntary feelings that grab us in the pit of our stomach? Why do some guys reach girls, while others do not? Why can some girls buckle a guy's knees, while others—equally attractive—don't do anything for him?

Is the answer simply that "love makes the world go round"? I don't think so. These pit-of-the-stomach feelings really have very little to do with love. Love sometimes happens after all the romantic ups and downs have run their course. So those exciting feelings are not really "love"; they are the expectation of possible love— they are the excitement just before the storm arrives.

All of us have seen pictures of the little chubby cherub who supposedly flies around, shooting romantic arrows at people. Because most of us have had sudden experiences of being attracted to someone of the opposite sex, we can relate to that little guy shooting people with arrows. When desire hits, it's just like being shot.

Romance is not love; it is the prelude to love. It is what happens in the beginning of many lasting relationships. Romance also is what keeps love's fires burning later, when stability— and perhaps boredom—have begun to set in. Romance helps to make a married couple's sex life more satisfying. Without romance there usually will be no love.

But romance also is dangerous. It is the fire in a relationship, but it can burn you. It is that uncontrollable geyser of feelings that overwhelms your reason and makes you do silly things for the one you love. It turns your head upside down and can cause you to do things for which you may be eternally sorry.

Now, more than ever before, involvement with the opposite sex is risky for teenagers. Fatal "love diseases" like AIDS and conflicting ideas of what is right and wrong can confuse you. If you listen to the sexual messages being preached through your television set, read typical teenage romance novels, or copy what your friends are doing, you may end up with major problems.

This book will help you discover what God wants your romantic life to be. You've got real desires and you need honest and healthy answers. It is my wish to expose you to a healthy way of enjoying romance and love.

This Thing Called "Romance"

"Romance" is a word that covers a lot of ground. Look it up in an unabridged dictionary and you'll see that the term is used for everything from having sex to being naive. Romance can be the ability to convince people of something that is really not true. It can be something idealistic and unrealistic. It can be the way a person exaggerates or invents detail in an incident. It can even be used to describe a group of languages, or fun activities like photography, music, and art. If you were asked to do something "romantic" for a member of the opposite sex, what would you do? Being "romantic" is often a difficult assignment. We all perceive it differently.

Being "romantic" is often a difficult assignment. We all perceive it differently.

Just talking about this subject makes most girls excited—and most guys bored. Why? Because romance is a special way of feeling, and many girls prefer to think about such feelings. Guys, on the other hand, usually don't like to think about the *process* of love; they don't have much desire to analyze their feelings. They usually prefer to think about the girl of their dreams rather than why they feel the way they do.

So what *is* romance? It is what makes us excited about the opposite sex. When someone touches us romantically, they attract us. We become intrigued, interested, and possibly even aroused. You don't have to understand romance to be affected by it.

Romance isn't just about being sexy. Romance is doing nice things for someone special, those little touches that show a person why he or she means so much to you. Being romantic is focusing on making someone else's life important to you.

In this Campus Magazine, we will examine the interesting and complex subject of romance from many different angles. Our goal is to help you see your feelings, your desires, and your relationships from the perspective of the One who invented love. My prayer is that when you are done with this magazine you will have a better understanding of how you can fulfill your God-given desires in righteous, healthy, and enjoyable ways. ♡

one

*T*hat Special Way o

Feeling

The Importance of Feelings

I looked across the room at Sharon and my heart ached. She was the best-looking girl I knew. She had a special way of talking to the girl in the seat in front of her—it just made me weak inside. I found it difficult to keep from staring. I hoped no one noticed.

We were in fifth grade. I distinctly remember thinking, *This isn't puppy love. This is the real thing. I know what I want.* I could picture myself married to Sharon, and often asked God if she was "the one." Sometimes, in my childishness, I would ask God to flash a big "Yes!" or a "No!" on the wall if Sharon was *the one* for me. I'd squint my eyes as hard as I could to see that "Yes" sign.

My crush on Sharon lasted well into junior high school. Every time I saw her, my stomach dropped to my knees. I "loved" her so intensely, I was never able to talk to her. Even after high school, when we had our first real conversation, I didn't let on that some of the magic was still there.

Feelings of romantic love can be the most enjoyable and the most painful of all emotions. They are a little like standing in front of a strong heat source in a cold room. You know your outside is getting roasted while your insides are still cold, but because you are so cold, you stand there anyway. You overdo it, fearing that if you pull away, you'll still be cold.

Feelings are important. (The Campus Magazine *Moods* covers that subject). Feelings are what make your life livable.

Feelings are what make your life livable.

Not having feelings means not living. This probably is why it has been said that it is better to have loved and lost a relationship with someone than never to have loved at all.

Archaeologists unearthed a four-thousand-year-old fragment of a clay tablet "love letter" in Babylon. The cuneiform inscription reads, "To Bibiya, I have come to Babylon and saw you not. Oh, I am so sad." In ancient Egypt, a woman separated from her lover wrote these bittersweet words on a shred of papyrus: "I go for a walk and you are with me in every beautiful place, and my hand is in your hand." Times and places may change, but feelings have been the same for thousands of years.

Deep feelings for someone of the opposite sex often come quickly, unannounced, and without our permission. These feelings must be controlled, but certainly not denied. If you feel strongly toward someone, it's okay.

Just learn to accept your emotions, knowing that they may well change.

At the turn of the century, a man named John Watson defined the feeling of love as "an innate emotion elicited by cutaneous stimulation of the erogenous zones" (in other words, it is something we can't control). Andreas Capellanus, in the twelfth century, defined it as "a certain inborn suffering derived from the sight of or excessive meditation upon the beauty of the opposite sex."

Strong love feelings are like a powerful heat source. Too much of a good thing can be deadly. But we must not run from all heat. Instead, we must learn how to get warm without getting burned.

This Thing Called Romance

Romance is . . .
- Anything that ends in a wedding.
- A relationship that is 1 percent sense and 99 percent sensation.
- A courtship during which a girl usually "whines" a man around her finger.
- An attachment that begins with give and take, and ends with misgive and mistake.
- A short period when two people cannot see enough of each other, followed by a long period when they see too much.

QuiZ

The Right & Wrong Approach

Questions (true or false):

1. When a man approaches a girl he doesn't know, it is best to sit down beside her rather than in front of her.

2. When a guy first meets a girl, the best way for him to start a relationship is to talk about himself so that the girl will know what kind of guy he is.

3. If a guy wants to gain a girl's interest, he should be willing to tell jokes at his own expense.

4. Playing hard to get is really effective in getting the interest of the opposite sex.

5. Because women are less attracted on the physical level, it doesn't matter too much how a guy fixes himself up.

6. Love is more likely to develop quickly with someone who is just an acquaintance rather than someone you know well.

Answers:

1. **False.** Where you sit when trying to meet someone has a lot of impact on the future of any relationship. Recent research shows that women tend to dislike men who sit at their sides, while they don't mind it when men sit opposite them. For some reason, for men, the opposite is true. Sitting beside a strange man is okay, but sitting opposite him tends to be more threatening.

2. **False.** Talking about his opinions and listing his assets (whether that's talking about his car, his apartment, his job, or his talents) in an attempt to impress a lady is foolish. A guy is more likely to gain her interest by encouraging her to talk about herself.

3. **False.** Although almost everyone likes a sense of humor, studies conducted at Indiana University indicate that when men told jokes that put themselves down, women found them less confident, less intelligent, and less witty. Whatever you do, resist the temptation to make the girl the butt of your jokes. The best form of humor is based on something neutral.

4. **True.** Playing hard to get tends to arouse interest in both sexes. It is human nature to want what you are not supposed to have, or what you cannot reach.

5. **False.** Physical attractiveness does play a big part in attracting a girl to a guy. Studies done at the University of Wisconsin have shown that the more attractive a man makes himself, the more likely he is to be seen as a desirable person.

6. **False.** The better you know someone, the more likely it is that he or she will already be interested in you. You will tend to be attracted to someone you are around the most. Church, school, the office, and other places where you spend a lot of time are likely places for this to happen.

Special Moments

"*T*he time is right, your perfume fills my head, the stars are red, and oh the night's so blue, and then I go and spoil it all by saying something stupid, like 'I love you.'" That song* sums up those moments when everything seems romantic and "right" but then you blow it.

If you really care about someone, you want to spend extra time—and "special moments"—with them. Special moments are a romantic phenomenon. They come and go when everything is right, and often include beautiful music, pleasant smells, sunsets, dim lights, loving words, tender

*"Somethin' Stupid" by C. C. Parks, BMI.

touches, long moments of seclusion from the rest of the world, and a lack of tension.

Every relationship will have special moments when things just "click," but special moments don't last. They may feel so good, you convince yourself you can make them last. But even in relationships that move into marriage, those moments will come and go. As you begin to date more and more, it may become obvious that you can have those exciting times with many different people. The danger comes when you begin to trust the moments and try to build your life around them.

A girl who gives of herself sexually because everything is "so romantic" soon realizes that what may have made it so exciting was sexual tension. That's the tenseness you feel when you desire to do more than you should. But when you give in to your body's cravings, you discover that the mystery and anticipation is gone. The excitement, mystique, and respect disappear. In their place comes overwhelming desire to repeat and surpass the sexual feelings you experienced earlier. Soon sex is your main reason for getting together; it begins to dominate and strangle your relationship. A date becomes nothing more than an excuse for "making out."

Don't be fooled by brief moments that promise heaven on earth. Truly special moments lead to sweet memories. If they lead instead to mutual sexual exploitation and guilty memories, they can be the death of your relationship.

Kiss & Tell

- Sign posted in a bank: "Don't kiss our girls; they're all tellers!"

- In Ancient Rome, a law stated that any virgin who could prove she had been kissed would be awarded full marriage rights.

Tired of sitting
Are you lonely

home alone?
again tonight?

Then you need *Romance*—
the perfume that draws men like bees to honey.
We've formulated this powerful fragrance with a
secret ingredient that laboratory experiments
have proven males can't resist.
Put *Romance* behind your ears,
and any boy you get close to
will irreversibly fall in love with you.

A little[1] *Romance* never hurt
any girl's love life.

Romance
The Irreversible Fragrance

How Romantic Are You?

As she sat at the lunch table next to her best friend, Karen Wells sighed an other-worldly, dazed sigh. A slow, almost sickly smile, grew on her face. Her friend didn't know whether she was tired, sick, or just in love.

"What's with you?" Sandy asked, trying to find out the reason for the distant expression on Karen's face.

"Oh, I went out with Chet last night. . . ." Her voice trailed away.

"And—?" Sandy asked.

"He is the most romantic boy I've ever known," Karen replied with a saccharine smile.

"So what does that mean? Did you guys have sex?"

"Oh, no, no. He was just so sweet, and . . . you know what I mean. He was just so romantic."

*G*etting Karen to explain her feelings was like trying to pick up a melting ice cube with a pair of hot chop sticks. She really couldn't put her finger on what it was that Chet had done, but she knew that she was absolutely mesmerized by his romanticism.

What makes a person "romantic?" I'm sure there are as many different answers to that question as there are people, but let's take a stab at it.

Romance is a feeling; it is doing things the way they "feel best" to you. A romantic person loves to give (and to receive) those unique little touches that make an evening important and special. Such "touches" may be opening car doors, pouring another person's beverage, helping take a coat off, wearing a nice fragrance, fixing up one's appearance, planning a date night so that everything is perfect, or buying an unexpected gift.

If you think about it, romantic activities are the things you do to make another person happy. They involve time and attention and thoughtfulness. These activities take effort in order to be successful. Part of romance is working at making someone else happy.

But let's face it. Your efforts won't always work. There are members of the opposite sex whom we try to woo with flowers and candy and love notes, and anything else we can think of—but they see our efforts to be romantic as a turnoff. Sometimes romance itself is a turnoff. This is especially true if the object of our affections hasn't shown any interest in us.

Romantic activities must be entered into slowly, lest we drive away the very person we were hoping to attract. No one likes to feel she is being chased by an overeager suitor. Part of successful romance is a sense of reserve that says, in essence, "I am giving you a part of me, but there is much more hidden below the surface if you care to find it." As strange as it might seem, there usually must be a sense of teasing or holding back. Give too much too soon, and you destroy what you are trying to build.

The same holds true for relationships that have been in existence for a while. Too much of any good thing means destruction. If you overdo it, you can make the relationship tiresome. We never want anything that doesn't keep us guessing at least a little bit. The fear of losing something is one of the big reasons for continued attraction.

Because romance is feeling-oriented, it is fragile. It can be destroyed quickly by too much or too little attention. The right mix depends on the people involved and, unfortunately, on the other possibilities on those people's horizons. ♡

Kissing in the Movies

- The first screen kiss recorded for commercial entertainment was performed by May Irwin and John C. Rice for a 30-second nickelodeon production. The couple's kiss was filmed, in 1896, in close-up for Vitascope. Herbert Stone, a Chicago publisher, complained that the film was "absolutely disgusting" and "indecent in its emphasized vulgarity. Such things call for police interference."

- In the James Bond film *Gold Finger* (United Artists, 1964), Bond (played by Sean Connery) kissed a sultry young woman named Bonita. In the middle of the kiss, 007 saw the reflection of an approaching killer in Bonita's pupils. (Apparently spies don't close their eyes when kissing.) Bond whirled with the woman still in his grasp, in time for the thug's blow to fall on her.

- After kissing Marilyn Monroe for the movie *Some Like It Hot* (United Artists, 1959), actor Tony Curtis complained that kissing her was "like kissing Hitler."

- When Rhett Butler (Clark Gable) kissed Scarlett O'Hara (Vivien Leigh) in the classic film *Gone With the Wind*, Leigh complained that Gable had bad breath.

- In the two versions of the movie *Invasion of the Body Snatchers*, the hero discovered through a kiss that his girlfriend's body had been taken over by an alien power.

**"The magic of first love is our ignorance that it can never end."
—Benjamin Disraeli**

Quiz

Romance in the Bible

How much do you know about romance in the Bible? Take the following quiz and see for yourself:

1. Who fell in love at first sight but worked fourteen years to get his girl?

2. Who saw a girl and asked his parents to get her for him?

3. What girl won a beauty contest in which the prize was marriage to a king?

4. What girl got courtship advice from her mother-in-law?

5. What guy spurned the advances of a married woman, only to be thrown into prison by her husband?

6. What is the most romantic book in the Bible?

7. What woman fell in love with foreigners after seeing their pictures?

8. Who loved a girl so much that he became sick?

9. What man had the most experience with members of the opposite sex?

10. What forty-year-old bachelor finally married two women who caused his parents nothing but grief?

"Take away leisure
and Cupid's bow is broken."
—Ovid

1. Jacob. (See Genesis 29:9-30.)

2. Samson. (See Judges 14:1-4.)

3. Esther. (See Esther 2.)

4. Ruth. (See Ruth 2–4.)

5. Joseph. (See Genesis 39.)

6. Song of Solomon.

7. Oholibah. She represents Jerusalem lusting after the Assyrians in a parable told by Ezekiel. (See Ezekiel 23:11-17.)

8. Amnon for Tamar, his sister. (See 2 Samuel 13:2.)

9. Solomon. He had 700 wives and 300 concubines! (See 1 Kings 11:3.)

10. Esau. (See Genesis 26:34-35.)

What's in a Flower?

I had purchased my first flower. It was a single, long-stemmed red rose that had cost me 50 cents, plus tax. I was a little fearful of giving it, as I was afraid that the recipient of my gift might feel it was silly, or even too forward.

I picked up Carolyn at her dorm in downtown Los Angeles, and when we got to the car, I unveiled the flower that I had hidden in the backseat. I couldn't believe her reaction. She smiled; she hugged me; she kissed me. It was her first flower. She wanted to wear it, but because it was long-stemmed, she settled for pinning it to the car visor so she could look at it while we drove.

I remember thinking, *What an investment. I can't believe she likes it so much! I'm going to have to do this more often.*

What is it about flowers, anyway, that make girls so happy? No matter how hard we try, I don't think we guys will ever understand why girls make such a big deal over them. Flowers just don't do it for us. We are made differently. Many guys have a hard time letting go of their hard-earned cash for something so temporary. They would prefer to give artificial flowers. That way, the gift can be appreciated longer, right? They would rather take a girl out to eat, give her candy, or buy her some jewelry to wear because flowers don't seem to have any lasting value. Even after couples are married, it is difficult for guys to think about getting their wives flowers—they are so easy to forget.

But it's the very fact that the flowers will fade away, I think, that makes them special. Girls love the fact that a boy is willing to buy something so frivolous for them. They are a fragile bit of color, fragrance, and natural beauty that says, "I care enough about you to waste some of my precious money on these petals that I know will be gone in just a matter of days."

Other than that, will males ever really figure out what's so special about flowers? Probably not.

Interesting Marriage Customs

- Once a year, the Incas of Peru gathered all the young men and maidens in their villages into facing rows. Then, in the name of the emperor, the priests and chieftains arbitrarily assigned a girl to each man.

- In the Greek city-state of Sparta, to encourage population growth and provide new recruits for its armies, marriage was virtually compulsory. Bachelors were heavily penalized. When all else failed, the authorities would round up a random group of single men and women and force them into a small dark room where each man had to pick a partner in the dark.

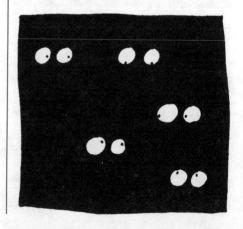

- In law books attributed to Manu in the second and third centuries, it says that the ideal marriage in India was considered to be between a bride who was eight years old and a groom who was 24. Although an eight-year-old bride would not live with her husband until she had reached puberty at the age of about twelve, the maturity difference between twelve and twenty-eight was vast indeed. The age difference meant that there were many widows who were not allowed to remarry and who suffered a harsh existence. No wonder many chose to die on their husbands' fiery funeral pyre.

- Imilchil, Morocco has a "marriage mart" each year. Every single man and woman eligible for marriage gathers for three days atop a 10,000-foot mountain for a mass wedding ceremony. As many as 15,000 have joined in the massive wedding dance.

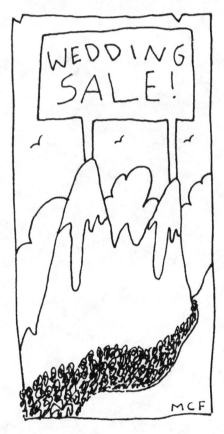

Who Are More Romantic: Men or Women?

"*R*eal Men Don't Eat Quiche" says the title of a well-known book. There still seems to be a conviction in the world today that certain things are unacceptable for macho men to do. Real men are not supposed to be emotional and would never show their feelings. They are not supposed to be sentimental or nostalgic. They should never carry on meaningful dialogues with members of the opposite sex. In short, they are supposed to project only a strong, in-control persona and do only "manly" things.

It also seems to most of us that women are far more romantic than men. Women tend to be the ones who cry at movies, get googly-eyed with little babies, and in general, embarrass their male friends with their sentimental feelings. The interesting thing is that in almost all studies on the subject of romanticism, it is the men who emerge as starry-eyed romantics!

A thousand college students between the ages of eighteen and twenty-four were asked, "If a man (or woman) had all the other qualities that you desire, would you marry this person if you were not in love with him (or her)?" Two out of every three men answered with a strong no. But more than three out of every four women said they would. It appeared that more men than women believed love was essential to a relationship.

When men "fall in love" they often have an ecstatic emotional experience. The whole world looks bright and beautiful. All their senses seem alert.

When men "fall in love" they often have an ecstatic emotional experience.

But men are trained at an early age to disregard emotion. They distrust the vulnerability of feelings so much that they usually enter marriage only after those early heavy feelings have subsided.

When men suffer rejection, many experience a heartache more typically associated with women in love. They report having terrible yearnings, loss of appetite, a sense of disorientation, shaky hands, wild surmises, and even being on the edge of a nervous breakdown.

Many men do not like the feeling of being "out of control" when they fall in love. Because a man may worry that the female in his life will someday pull the plug on him, he may tend to look for a relationship in which the girl loves him more than he loves her.

The Royal and the Famous

- Isabella of Angouleme invited King John of England to her wedding. When the monarch saw her, on August 24, 1200, he decided she was too good to be true. So he kidnapped her and married her himself. Sixteen years later, after the king had died, she married her original beau, Count Hugh.
- In 1297, after a two-year engagement, Princess Isabelle de Valois was jilted by Prince Edward of Scotland. She was immediately married to Duke Jean III, who was eleven. The princess was only four years old.

Quiz

Are You Romantic or Realistic?

Are you a romantic or a realist? To find out, take the following quiz. Next to the list of questions below, record the letter that best describes how you feel about the guy or girl of your dreams, whether or not he or she is currently in your life.

1. If you are in love with someone:
   a. you should be able to confide in him/her about anything.
   b. there will always be things that you cannot confide to him/her.

2. When you're in love, your girlfriend's (or boyfriend's) faults:
   a. shouldn't be overlooked because they might eventually sabotage your relationship.
   b. are not even seen, and if they are, they are easily overlooked.

3. The attractiveness of your boyfriend (or girlfriend) is:
   a. very important to the future of the relationship. If you don't think he/she's attractive, it can't last.
   b. not that important, because beauty is only skin deep. Other qualities are more important to a long-term relationship.

4. If there are major obstacles to your relationship:
   a. true love will overcome them all.
   b. it's important to deal with each obstacle or it could ruin the relationship.

5. True love comes:
   a. only once—maybe twice—during a lifetime.
   b. many times during the course of a lifetime.

6. When love comes, it:
   a. just happens. One minute it's not there, and the next, you're madly in love.
   b. develops gradually as you become more familiar with someone.

7. When I'm in love, it:
   a. affects me, but not enough for me to lose control over my emotions.
   b. affects my judgment so that I'm liable to do erratic and unpredictable things.

8. For every person, there:
   a. is one ideal mate. The problem is to find that person.
   b. are many possible lifetime partners. You must choose yours carefully.

9. I enjoy being with my girlfriend (or boyfriend):
   a. as often as I can.
   b. often, but I also enjoy my times of being alone.

10. If I was dumped by my ideal boyfriend (girlfriend):
   a. it would hurt, but I would recover.
   b. I don't think I could ever get over it

Answers:

Romantic answers: **1a, 2b, 3a, 4a, 5a, 6a, 7b, 8a, 9a, 10b.**
Realistic answers: **1b, 2a, 3b, 4b, 5b, 6b, 7a, 8b, 9b, 10a.**

How to score yourself: For every "romantic answer" you marked, give yourself one point. When you have totalled your points, read on for a description of your personality type.

The Complete Romantic (8 to 10 points)—This person places a high value on emotions and believes that feelings are the best guide for living a successful life. As amazing as it might seem, surveys show that there are more men in this category than women.

When the romantic meets a person of the opposite sex, he either loves or hates the person immediately. When he falls in love, he daydreams, acts erratically, and gazes longingly into his loved one's eyes. To the romantic, love is exciting and endlessly fascinating.

The Rational Romantic (5 to 7 points)—This type of person is still very much a romantic, but views things with a little more realism. He likes to do all the romantic activities, but is not as likely to get paranoid about his loved one's outside activities as the complete romantic might. He believes a sense of balance is necessary to keep a relationship healthy.

The Romantic Rationalist (3 to 4 points)—This person is much more rational in his approach to life than even the Rational Romantic. He tends to analyze everything in terms of cause and effect, but still can be moved emotionally. He believes that most successful relationships are founded on mutual consideration and sharing. He is interested in the emotional stability of his partner.

Because this type of person does not get as emotionally involved in a marriage relationship as other types, he may not feel as happy. Secular studies seem to show that this personality is more likely to have extramarital affairs when he encounters someone who moves him more than the stable person he married.

The Extreme Realist (0-2 points)—This person sees life only through realistic glasses. Emotions never get the better of his intellect. He likes a strong partner who is as independent as he is. He has trouble understanding passionate people. He may not sweep you off your feet, but he makes an excellent long-term companion. ♡

Unrequited Love

"To find yourself jilted is a blow to your pride.
Do your best to forget it, and if you don't succeed,
at least pretend to."
—Moliere

Silly Romance

An unmarried girl is a lot like a baseball player.
She's always trying to stretch a single into a double.

A girl to her fiancé getting a marriage license:
"Seems silly to get the license after the hunting is over."

"Why are you chasing her?"
Shirley's father asked the neighbor's son
as the little boy chased Shirley around the porch.
"Because she pinched me," responded the boy.
"Why did you pinch him?" he asked his daughter.
"So he would chase me," she replied sheepishly.

A young girl quit her job as a secretary
to marry her boss, a rich oil man.
"He's everything I've dreamed of," she confided to a girl friend.
"He's tall, dark, and has some."

Is He Romantic?

You know that a guy is feeling romantic
when he wants to call a girl by his last name.

Quiz

What Is Your Body Saying?

1. What does your body language show?

2. When two people of the opposite sex look at each other "too long," what does it signal?

3. What does it mean when eye contact is made with a stranger of the opposite sex, followed by a smile?

4. How can you know when someone is listening to you with approval?

5. What is a person saying when he sits rigidly, with his shoulders slightly forward, and his arms clasped in front?

6. Does touching usually help build or tear down trust?

7. Is it possible to change your attitude by changing your body language?

Answers:

1. Did you know that your body talks? Body language is the way you hold yourself. It is an outward expression of what you are feeling on the inside. You may think to yourself, "No, I'm not like that. I don't feel that way." But your body usually speaks more truthfully than your words. It can reveal feelings you are not even conscious of.

2. There is a "moral looking time," which is the length of time you can hold someone's eye and still be within the bounds of propriety. When someone violates that by even a half second, a signal is sent. The message between members of the opposite sex is, "I am interested in you."

The moral looking time is different for every situation. In an elevator, it is almost nonexistent. When giving a speech, eye contact can be much longer. Each of us either knows, or soon learns, the amount of time we can look at someone before others start to wonder what it is we're saying.

3. Eye contact followed by a smile generally says, "I'm interested in you. I'd like to talk to you." Many young people think that smiling might not be "cool." Yet, a smile tells the opposite sex that you like them, that you approve of them, that you'd like to get to know them.

4. They nod at you. Almost everyone, instinctively, nods in approval during a conversation, to signal that they're listening and that they agree with what you're saying. If you don't receive those little nods, you may feel as though you're talking to a stone wall and lose interest.

5. A person who sits in this closed posture is giving the impression that he is tight, rigid, and above all, inaccessible. Knees closed together, arms pulled into the body, stiff back, and no smiles are all signs of someone who doesn't want to meet anyone. These also are symptoms of a nervous person. If you are nervous, yet want to meet new people, change your body posture to one that is more open and relaxed.

6. Inappropriate touching can violate another person's space, but it also can help build trust. In one experiment, a librarian was asked to accidentally touch book borrowers when she handed them their books. A researcher, stationed at the door, later asked the book borrowers about how they perceived the services of the library, and especially the librarian. Whenever she had allowed that little touch, no matter how brief, she was thought of as warmer and more understanding than when she didn't.

You can spot a relationship that has been established for some time because the partners will touch each other a lot. Touching can show rights of possession. If you are a Christian, it is important to keep touching to the level appropriate for each relationship. Touching that gets out of control will encourage inappropriate sexual involvement. A couple who hangs all over each other in public are involved in inappropriate touching.

7. Yes. If you realize that you are cutting someone off by the way you are standing (arms crossed over your chest, head back at a critical angle), and you don't want to appear unfriendly, you can change your body posture to a more open and relaxed position and thus change your attitude toward the person to whom you are talking.

A Romantic Sense of Smell?

How romantic is your sense of smell? Think about it. It's not as stupid as it sounds. Smells play a large part in the game of romance.

*I*n 1959 German researchers borrowed the Greek word *pheromone* (which means "to transfer excitement") to describe a strong sexual attractant found in animals, insects, and humans. Many insect and animal species rely on this odor to communicate their desire to mate. When the female gypsy moth, for example, is ready to mate, she sends out her unique pheromone, and the males, sensing the smell with their antennae, flock to her from miles away.

Animals use scent signals to mark territory, send out alarms, issue angry warnings, show aggression, and attract mates. In some cases, the male secretes a pheromone that makes the female start her estrous cycle and become ready for mating. The sexual reaction of animals to odor is so universal that farmers can purchase an aerosol product that contains an artificial pheromone in order to ready a sow for mating.

A few years ago, a successful advertising campaign for a soap invented the term "B.O." (body odor) to urge people to get rid of their human odors. We wash all our smells away, and then use deodorants to mask our natural scents even further.

But, interestingly enough, perfume companies discovered that certain perfumes, when mixed with the natural pheromones of animals (e.g., musk from the musk deer, civet from the civet cat, and catoreum from the beaver) triggered a strong sexual attraction. Now many perfumes and toilet waters are laced with these animal pheromones.

It might seem gross, but in the past, when people washed less often than we do today, men would often expose women to a handkerchief from their armpits. The Victorian lady, hoping to catch a gentleman's attention, often kept her handkerchief in her bodice before dropping it in his path. The odors tended to arouse desires in the opposite sex. Many people have found themselves strangely attracted to someone because of their scent.

We are accustomed to thinking of body odor as a real turn-off, but it can also be a turn-on. Mixed with the aroma of perfumes and after-shaves, everyone's smell is different. If we don't like how someone smells, chances are good we will find it hard to like them as well.

Never underestimate the effect of smell to your romantic consciousness. Obvious fragrances like perfumes and after-shave lotions can encourage interest and embellish special moments that become lasting memories. Things like the smell of a roaring fire on the beach, or the aroma of a meal prepared for you by someone you care about, can go a long way toward intensifying your feelings of love. ♥

Love "Quotas"

"Love, in distinction from friendship, is killed, or rather extinguished, the moment it is displayed in public." —Hannah Arendt

"Love is not love until love's vulnerable." —Theodore Roethke

"Only little boys and old men sneer at love." —Louis Auchincloss

How Do I Love Thee?

Ann Morrow Lindbergh wrote of her first sight of Charles Lindbergh: "I saw standing against the great stone pillar . . . a tall boy in evening dress . . . so much slimmer, so much taller, so much more posed than I had expected. A very refined face . . . a firm mouth, clear, straight blue eyes, fair hair, and nice color."

Composer Robert Schumann wrote to his fiancée, Clara Wieck, "Once you were in a black dress, going to the theater. . . . I know you will not have forgotten; it is vivid with me. . . . And yet another time, as you were putting on your hat after a concert, our eyes happened to meet, and yours were full of the old unchanging love. I picture you in all sorts of ways, as I have seen you since."

"Don't you think I was made for you?" Zelda Fitzgerald asked author F. Scott Fitzgerald shortly after they met. *"I feel like you had me ordered— and I was delivered to you."*

Napoleon Bonaparte was in battle headquarters when he wrote to Josephine, "I have not spent a day without loving you; I have not spent a night without embracing you; I have not so much as drunk a single cup of tea without cursing the pride and ambition which force me to remain separated from the moving spirit of my life. In the midst of my duties . . . my beloved Josephine stands alone in my heart, occupies my mind, fills my thoughts. If I am moving away from you with the speed of the Rhone torrent, it is only that I may see you again more quickly. If I rise to work in the middle of the night, it is because this may hasten by a matter of days the arrival of my sweet love."

The Risk Factor

A man who was still single at eighty-one was asked why he never married. "Because I couldn't ever bear the idea of loving someone and then losing her. Suppose I committed myself to a woman and married her? Eventually I might run the risk of losing her through death or desertion. I couldn't stand that!"

Let's face it, entering into a relationship with the opposite sex means taking risks. We may be rejected, made a fool of, stood up, two-timed, used and abused, and gossiped about. Even trying to meet someone is a risk-taking proposition; our attempts at friendship can be put down before we even get started.

Still, I'm sure you will agree that it is better to love and lose than never to have a chance to love at all. What you miss by not taking risks is far worse than what you suffer if a lover leaves you.

Life is full of risks. And really the more you are willing to take risks, the more chances you will have of achieving success in life. If you do not attempt anything, you will not accomplish anything. Throw some of your cautions to the wind and get involved with life.

Notice I said *some* of your cautions. It is wise to be careful in your risk-taking with the opposite sex. For instance, if a girl gets asked out by an attractive guy who has a reputation as a big wolf on campus, wisdom says she should turn the date down. If she says no, the chances are likely that she will: 1) save herself a lot of grief; and 2) show him he can work on changing his reputation if he wants to go out with her badly enough.

Dating is not a time to experiment with your standards. If you don't know where you stand on the issue of sex, for instance, it is highly likely that you will end up in bed with someone you are not married to. Don't take serious risks that have a high probability of failure. Stick to risks that have a high possibility of success.

Let's suppose a guy notices a girl who has a tremendous testimony and walk with the Lord and a social circle much different from his own. It is risky for him to try to enter into her world, but that risk is worth taking because he is attempting to develop a relationship that will encourage his own spirituality. This is a risk of upward growth.

Take risks that God would have you take. A good question to ask yourself is, "If I fail in this challenge, what kind of effect will it have on me and my relationship with God?" If the rejection will have a debilitating effect, perhaps it's not worth the chance. But if a risk will definitely cause you to grow through a failure, it might be worth pursuing.

Sexual Stats

- How much of a couch potato are you? In ten years of TV watching, a typical viewer will see 90,000 scenes indicating that sex has taken place. Of these incidences, 72,000 will be outside of marriage.

- Of 1,400 Christian kids surveyed, 45 percent said they had engaged in sexual intercourse. Thirty-six percent did not believe that it was wrong to have sex before marriage.

- During the next twenty-four hours more than 35,000 Americans will contract a sexually transmitted disease (STD). That means 13 million people will get an STD in the next year! A few years ago, there were only five major diseases; today there are thirty-four. One of these, AIDS, is fatal.

Love Not Spoken Here

Until just a few years ago, the definition for the word "love" was left out of dictionaries in the People's Republic of China. Love was seen as a "decadent bourgeois silliness," not worthy of a definition.

three

In Love with Love

Cynthia was one of those girls who always seem to have stars in her eyes. She enjoyed being around guys so much that each new boyfriend was the man of her dreams. Her friends, who had watched her "fall in love" with losers, got tired of warning her that each boyfriend was "a big mistake." They figured she would just have to learn the hard way.

Cynthia didn't want to look too closely at a guy's character because she was afraid she might find something wrong. She wanted a boyfriend so badly she was willing to overlook the "little things." She tended to create a "cover" for each new guy who came along until his bad character eventually destroyed their relationship. Somehow, Cynthia didn't seem to learn her lesson. She moved in and out of relationships with the same kind of guy, attracted to the losers like a moth to an open flame. She just knew that some day her "bad luck" would end and she would find somebody who was as loving and faithful as she was. Eventually she married Jack, who drank ("just a little bit") and smoked pot ("but he wasn't hooked").

Even after she discovered the real extent of Jack's problems, Cynthia continued to make excuses for him. But the fact that her husband didn't like to work made life more and more difficult. Sure, he had moments of employment, but he was never really happy with any job or boss for long. He would either quit, get fired, or just stay home for no real reason. He finally gave up all interest in employment.

This put Jack and Cynthia and their young children on welfare. And, because Jack was content to sit around with his friends drinking and smoking pot, not really caring if the children were fed or clothed, it also put the burden for the family's well-being on Cynthia.

Why did Cynthia end up in this predicament? More than any other reason, because she had been in love with love. She wasn't willing to be choosy about whom she married. Her Christian beliefs had no teeth to them. Sure, she took the kids to church, but what she believed didn't seriously change her life. She had little Christian impact on her husband because being in love and getting married were more important to her than what the Lord wanted.

Do you have the potential to become another "Cynthia?" Are you in love with love more than you are in love with the Lord? If the Lord asked you

Are you in love with love more than you are in love with the Lord?

to break up with a guy (perhaps speaking through your parents), are the chances good that the guy—not the Lord—would be the winner? Perhaps you'd just date the guy secretly?

"For whoever wishes to save his life shall lose it," Jesus said (Luke 9:24a). If you want your own way, and refuse to listen to what God wants for you, you'll have to live with your own choices.

If, on the other hand, you desire to live for the Lord, he promises that " . . . whoever loses his life for My sake, he is the one who will save it" (Luke 9:24b). Losing your life means daily giving up your desires and asking the Lord to take control (Luke 9:23). In the long run—or short run— it is a far better, safer, and happier way to live.

Increase Your Lovability!

(for only $9.95[1])

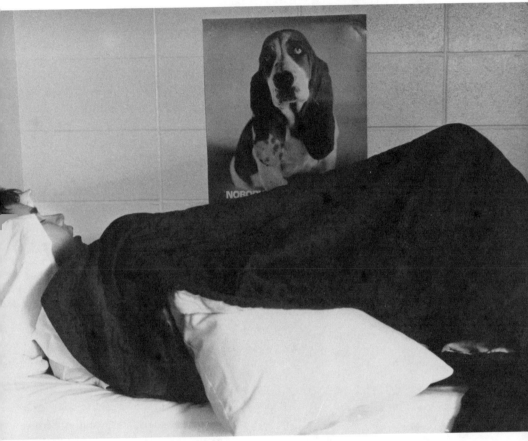

Do you feel about as romantic as a pet rock? Are you sometimes accused of being a member of the "nerd herd"? Take heart! Now there is a foolproof way to get members of the opposite sex to fall in love with you. You won't believe the thrilling results that anyone can achieve with the helpful suggestions[2] in our brain-mesmerizing program.

This scientifically proven[3] method for your success is contained on a cassette with hidden[4] subliminal messages. Simply place the tape in your recorder under your pillow at night. While sleeping, you'll be transformed into a truly adorable, lovable human being.

Just think, no more tiresome appointments with your dermatologist and your orthodontist. And no more diets! You won't need them with our program. With our amazing system there is no work and no bother—just a whole new you! So send $9.95 in cash, check, or money order to:

The Small Print:
[1] Your payment of $9.95 represents your agreement to pay the entire purchase price of $199.95. But don't worry, we'll bill you monthly for the difference.
[2] We don't, so we don't expect you to either.
[3] A former high school science student has successfully tested our program on himself in the laboratory. The chimps now love him!
[4] That means you can't hear anything when you listen to the tape.

Oh, Those Feelings

Romance is something that is anticipated with pleasure, experienced with problems, but remembered with nostalgia.

Debilitating Love

"When you fall in love with someone, you're finished. It's always like that!"
—Francoise Sagan

"As soon as you cannot keep anything from a woman, you love her."
—Paul Geraldy

"Most of us love from our need to love, not because we find someone deserving."
—Nikki Giovanni

"Love is the triumph of imagination over intelligence."
—H. L. Mencken

"Many a man has fallen in love with a girl in a light so dim he would not have chosen a suit by it."
—Maurice Chevalier

Sexual Chemistry

Ammie Jennings, a single girl, was dancing at a singles' bar when a waltz was announced. She decided to sit that one out, when suddenly a man whom she had not seen before appeared and asked her to dance.

She turned to him, ready to refuse, until their eyes met. Without warning, her heart began to race, her knees became weak, and she had trouble speaking. She could see in his eyes that whatever had hit her had also hit him. Instead of dancing, they sat down and engaged in an intimate conversation.

The man's name was James, and he quickly confessed that he was happily married with two children. He was in town on a business trip and would be leaving the next morning. Nothing serious could come of their relationship. Nevertheless, the sexual attraction between them was so strong, they went home to Ammie's apartment and spent the night. After that, they saw each other every time James was in town.

This kind of attraction usually is called "love at first sight." In this case, however, there definitely was no love. Both believed that their on-again off-again relationship would not affect James' marriage or Ammie's freedom. They were wrong—both were not only affected, but terribly damaged. Ultimately, James and Ammie parted—but not until they had cost each other, and James' family, a great deal of pain and grief. As wrong as they are, relationships like James and Ammie's are quite common today. A strong attraction between two people can cause them to have a sexual relationship without any commitments or love.

So many people think that "the right one" will come along, and that will be it; there won't be any feelings of attraction for anyone else. Unfortunately, that's often not the way things go. It is possible to be hit by a sexual attraction that makes you lose your inhibitions and do things you know are totally wrong—all because they are exciting and feel good.

Researchers have discovered that when two people are suddenly attracted to each other, their sympathetic nervous systems begin to create the hormone norepinephrine, which is released in the nerve endings and in the adrenal glands. Norepinephrine and another hormone, dopamine, affect the pleasure center in the brain and are directly responsible for what we feel when we "fall in love."

Such things as a rapid pulse, a compulsion to talk, a feeling of euphoria, and a comfortable ability to be bold with someone are all the result of chemical stimulation in our brains. We feel excitement, happiness, and a sense of anticipation when tiny electrical impulses occur in the brain's pleasure center.

A Yale University researcher working with a rhesus monkey implanted a tiny probe into the limbic system (the brain's pleasure center) and rigged up a device which allowed the

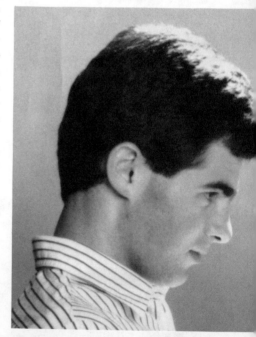

monkey to stimulate himself with a tiny electrical impulse by pressing a lever. The monkey would give up food and drink as long as he could be stimulated emotionally. If allowed, he literally would pleasure himself to death.

In the same way, our human response to the stimuli of an attractive person is the release of powerful natural drugs in our brain. The amphetamine-like substance that is released causes such a powerful pleasure sensation that we are likely to give up sleep and food and grow pale with love.

This attraction can be completely one-sided. You can have tremendous feelings for someone who doesn't even know you exist. But for true sexual "chemistry" to happen, there needs to be a response from the love object. When the person you are attracted to suddenly feels the same way, it's like two chemicals coming together to form an explosive compound. Suddenly the intense feelings are magnified by someone else who feels the same way you do. These feelings can be hard to control.

Now don't let this give you the impression that once those chemicals are released, we become prisoners to our strong sexual attractions. We *always* have a choice in the matter. Certainly, the feelings can be intense, but we can always decide what we're going to do about them. We can refuse to indulge feelings if they are too strong and for the wrong person.

True love grows over time. We may be attracted instantly to one another, but that attraction may or may not grow into what is a true, lifelong love relationship. Love is more than feelings and simple brain chemistry. After a couple have been married for some time, the original strong sexual chemistry changes; it seldom is the same as it was when they were first dating. A new form of attraction comes that results in a lifetime of commitment.

Love is more than feelings and simple brain chemistry.

Sexual attraction is an exciting part of our romantic lives, but we must beware of it. We can be fooled by those intense pleasurable feelings and become convinced that "this is it." We can begin to think that no one else could ever make us feel this way—when in reality, the feelings will happen many times.

This is why it is important to test your feelings over time. Watch them to see what will develop when you get to know the person better. Romantic attraction develops best in our minds, apart from the reality of what a person is really like. When you get to know someone better, you may discover that what turned you on at first doesn't affect you any more. In fact, it may turn you off.

Drugs and Romance

*P*henylethylamine, a chemical released by the body, is thought to be one of the stimulators of the brain that causes a person to become more susceptible to "falling in love." The excited flush that changes your entire outlook, the strong attraction for another person, the rising of your pulse, the heightened awareness of things, all make a person more capable of falling in love.

Apparently, amphetamines do some of the same things to the brain. One fellow—we'll call him Steve—confessed that he had been addicted to amphetamines as a young man. When he was high, he'd meet a girl at a bar or a dance and immediately be "in love." Later, he'd look at her and wonder what he had seen in her. Steve admitted this had happened many times.

No wonder sex and drugs go hand-in-hand! The more drugs you have, the more likely it is that your inhibitions will go down, and you may easily become involved with the wrong person, or even the right person before the proper time. Alcohol can have the same effect on a person. It increases the desire for sex, but decreases the ability to perform. If you want to remain in control of your sexual desires, avoid drugs and alcohol at all costs. ♡

What Kind of Love?

*R*ichard and Helen walked silently, side-by-side. They seldom looked at each other—they weren't even holding hands—but if you were observant, you could see that they were very attracted to each other. Not only did they care about one another, there was a deep sense of respect glowing between them. Richard was sixty-eight years old, and Helen was sixty-four.

The Beatles' song "When I'm Sixty-Four" has a young man asking a woman if she'll still love him when he's old and losing his hair. When we're dating, and a strong sexual attraction hits us with all of its accompanying physical and chemical reactions, we are certain it will last a lifetime. Then, amazingly, it passes. Or worse, it passes for our loved one and not for us. How can we be sure we'll be loved when we're sixty-four?

There are different kinds of love. The Greeks had a word for the kind of physical and sexual attraction we've been talking about so far. They called it *eros*. Eros is a love that is based upon sexual feelings for its survival and is therefore very fragile. If we are not loved in return, eros love will usually die.

Eros can be very selfish; it is easily offended and hurt; it can betray itself by switching to a new, more exciting love object. Eros' desire to be fulfilled can help it self-destruct. The greater its demands, the more likely it is that it will force the loved one into compromising sexually. Although it would be nice if every marriage had strong physical attraction present, eros is not a good love upon which to base a relationship.

Phileo is the word the Greeks used to describe nonromantic, tender affection from one person to another. It is love between friends. Most people don't want to "just be friends" with someone to whom they are attracted, but it is not a bad idea for lovers to be friends. If you don't consider your beau to also be a close friend, chances are good that there won't be much left to the relationship when the sexual attraction dies. Good, deep friendship makes for long-lasting marriages.

The third Greek word for love was *agape*. The Christian church took that word and used it to describe a kind of love very different from what most people normally experience. Agape love is God's love for men. It is a love that he injects into us once we invite Christ to come into our hearts. It becomes the kind of love that we are to have for everyone, including our romantic loved ones.

We love when others love us back.

To understand agape love, think for a moment about how God loves us. He loves us before we do anything to deserve it because love is his nature (1 John 4:8). He loved us enough to send his Son to die for us on the cross

(Romans 5:8). He keeps on loving us, in spite of what we're really like.

As you can see, this is not human love. We love when others love us back. We love because someone is worthy of our love. We love because we like the one we're loving. None of this is how God loves us, and it certainly isn't how he wants us to love others.

When we become Christians, we receive God's agape love because we receive Christ in our lives. It's as though we receive some of God's personality; we soon begin to exhibit it if we stay tuned to who he is. As Christians, we are to love one another with this self-sacrificial love.

Would you like to read more about agape love? Probably the best passage in the Bible to describe what agape love is all about is 1 Corinthians 13:1-8.

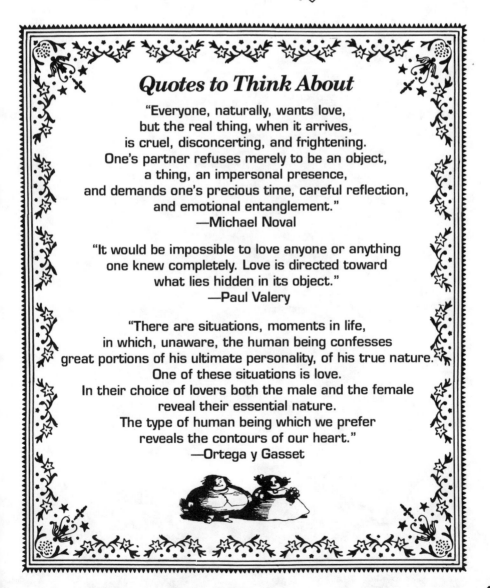

Quotes to Think About

"Everyone, naturally, wants love,
but the real thing, when it arrives,
is cruel, disconcerting, and frightening.
One's partner refuses merely to be an object,
a thing, an impersonal presence,
and demands one's precious time, careful reflection,
and emotional entanglement."
—Michael Noval

"It would be impossible to love anyone or anything
one knew completely. Love is directed toward
what lies hidden in its object."
—Paul Valery

"There are situations, moments in life,
in which, unaware, the human being confesses
great portions of his ultimate personality, of his true nature.
One of these situations is love.
In their choice of lovers both the male and the female
reveal their essential nature.
The type of human being which we prefer
reveals the contours of our heart."
—Ortega y Gasset

Is God like You?

"Don't you see? Man wasn't created by God in his own image," Phil began. "The reverse is really true. Man created God in his image. You see, man had the need for some higher power on whom to blame his problems. So he created God as a convenient way of covering for himself and the things he couldn't understand or explain. There is no God except in man's imagination."

I had to admit Phil's words made me stop and think. I had never heard any argument like this before. I was a high school senior, and still a relatively young Christian. What Phil said certainly seemed logical.

Phil was the star goalie of our high school water polo team. He was also a friend of Joe, one of my closest friends. As the three of us drove down the road, my mind was confused. I thought I should have some sharp log-ical answer for him, but none was coming. Then I thought about what I knew of Phil's moral life. He was sleeping with a fellow classmate's mother.

"You know, Phil, everything you've said is logical and makes sense—in its own context. But the problem I have with what you've said is where it has taken you. Because you feel there is no God, you have eliminated the need for morality. I look at your life, and it is the best argument against the logic of what you're suggesting. I don't want my life to become like yours. I'm afraid I can't accept your conclusions about God."

Phil just swore at me, but I learned something that night: a man's beliefs will help him justify his immorality, or keep him from it. Either our beliefs will change to fit our actions or we will bring our behavior in line with what we know is right.

If you have a moral dilemma, *you will* create God in your own image. In your mind, you'll create a God who understands your problems and accepts you and your sins without asking for any changes in your behavior. Phil had de-created God into a figment of man's imagination so that he could justify his own immorality.

In Psalm 50:21 God lists the sins of some evil people and then says that the reason they didn't understand their sins was because "you thought that I was just like you." We make a great mistake if we stray from the God of the Bible and instead believe in a wimpy Creator who does not care what we do.

Many couples get deeply involved in sexual immorality because they tell themselves that something that feels so good just couldn't be wrong. After all, they reason, God created sex. He knows the temptation and the struggles they're going through and therefore must approve of their sexual involvement with each other.

That might sound logical, but it is an argument created in self-deception. The Bible makes it quite plain that God considers such behavior an "abomination." That's a heavy word. God sees immorality and serving other gods as being about equal—he uses the same terms to describe both (see 1 Corinthians 6:9, 10). Therefore, if you reason that God doesn't care about your involvement in immorality, you've created a new God—one who is certainly not the God of the Bible.

If you are in love with love, you will want to believe unmarried sex is okay, even if God says it's wrong. You will want God to approve of your behavior because "it feels so good." But your first duty is to love the Lord your God with all of your heart, your mind, and your soul. If you start there, you won't have any trouble doing the will of the One who is revealed in the pages of the Bible.

Welcome to Fantasyland

*F*antasyland is supposed to be a place where dreams come true. But it is really the domain of unrealistic expectations, hopes, and dreams. It is not the real world; it is the world as we would have it, if we could call all the shots.

Fortunately, we can't control how everything turns out. If we could, we would quickly mess up everything. We think we know what's best for ourselves, but we choose only what feels the best. And feelings often lie to us.

We are fooled, believe it or not, because we want to be fooled. When we hear what we would like to hear, we often decide not to think too carefully for fear we will find some fault in the good news coming our way. We want it to be true so badly that we prefer not to know the truth if it will make us temporarily unhappy.

One of the secrets of staying out of trouble is to be certain you are not making foolish choices. Landlords check references to see what kind of a tenant a person has been in the past. Employers check on past employment history. Wouldn't it be nice if there was a "marriage credit bureau," which would tell you all about a person's character before you got married?

If there was such a bureau, most people wouldn't use it. We prefer to make our own mistakes and learn the hard way. We don't want to know the truth because we don't want our fantasies destroyed.

Maturity comes after we have made a few mistakes and have learned to be more careful when we make decisions. No one but a fool likes to make the same mistakes over and over again. Maybe this is what makes the American practice of dating useful. Hopefully you learn, by trial and error, about the pitfalls of developing a relationship with the opposite sex too quickly. Let's trust that you learn to be more careful and to take only worthwhile risks. (To learn more about risks, read the article called "The Risk Factor" in chapter 2.)

As long as you know that almost everyone has a tendency to live in Fantasyland, you can arm yourself with a questioning spirit. Remember, when something feels too good to be true, the chances are it *is* too good to be true.

How to Stay Out of Trouble

Only God knows what is best for us. That's why it's wise to listen to him so we won't fall into Fantasyland. Proverbs 3:5-6 says it well: "Trust in the LORD with all your heart and lean not on your own understanding; in all your ways acknowledge him, and he will make your paths straight" *(NIV)*. Take a look at each part of this passage and write down what you think it is saying.

1. "Trust in the LORD with all your heart"

_____

_____

2. "Lean not on your own understanding"

_____

_____

3. "In all your ways acknowledge him"

_____

_____

4. "And he will make your paths straight."

_____

_____

four

The Use and Abuse

Spotting the Pretender

Alice Pearson cuddled up to her boyfriend. This was their one-month anniversary. They had gone out five times, and each date had been more glorious than its predecessors.

Mike was so warm and lovable. He was the kind of guy Alice had always dreamed of finding. Her only problem was how she was going to wait for marriage. At sixteen, they were both too young. She had always envisioned herself finishing college before she got married, so the thought of tying the knot early did not appeal to her. But that meant she had to wait five years before she could get married.

She *knew* Michael was the right guy. He had recently come to her church and had a dramatic conversion. He wanted to be a missionary, and it *of* **Romance**

seemed that all of the girls in the youth group had a crush on him. Alice had been the lucky one he had chosen to form a relationship with.

"You know, I feel called to be a missionary," Mike began. "Would you ever consider being a missionary's wife?"

"Oh, Michael, of course I would!" Alice replied. "If the right missionary wanted me to be his wife, I'd jump at the chance."

"I was just thinking. If I am going to be all that God wants me to be, I am going to need a strong Christian girl . . . like you. Let's pray about it. I feel that the Lord just might be calling us to get married."

"Oh, Michael! I love you!" Alice said beaming, and then she embraced him. It seemed to her that they were getting so close; she had never known any boy in whom she could confide all her intimate thoughts.

As they grew closer, it just seemed natural for them to become more intimate physically. Soon they were doing so much that Alice was having a difficult time stopping. She knew it was wrong, yet it didn't really feel wrong. And after all, she told herself, they were going to get married.

Michael never pushed her. He was the perfect gentleman. But she could see how disappointed he would become whenever she stopped him. So she gave in one night. Soon she couldn't wait to have sex with Mike. This lasted for a month, until Alice heard a stirring Sunday morning sermon and became convicted that what they were doing was wrong. They needed to break off their sexual relationship to get back into God's will.

When Alice told Mike about her conviction, he broke up with her. She was devastated. She had given everything to this boy because she had believed they would one day be married. Now he was leaving her. What hurt the most was when he told her that he couldn't respect her anymore.

Then Alice had to watch as Michael started dating Mari, one of her better friends in the youth group. Over the next six months, she watched him systematically date all of the attractive girls in the group. From conversations she had with them after the relationships ended, Alice learned that he had managed to go to bed with all of them.

As painful as it was, Alice still loved Michael. He was the first and only boy she had ever given herself to, and although she felt betrayed, she found it hard not to love him from a distance. Even though she knew he had slept with others, she had to admit that she would probably go back with him if he ever came her way again.

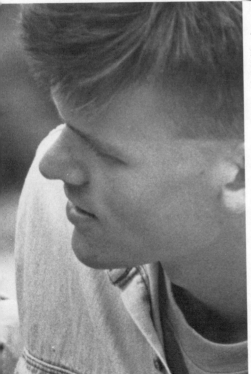

Amazingly, Mike's Christian reputation in the group somehow stayed intact. He continued to witness for the Lord and talked openly of his plans for missionary service. Meanwhile, the number of his ex-girlfriends continued to grow.

After Alice's conversations with the other "rejectees" in Mike's life, she had begun to wonder about his true spirituality. In each relationship Mike had lost respect for the girl after a period of sexual intimacy. And in each case, he didn't lose that respect until the girl stopped the sex.

In the end, Mike was confronted by their youth pastor. It came out, before he left the church, that he had never really been a Christian. He was a pretender who had heard that Christian girls were easy marks if you approached them from a religious angle.

How could so many Christian young

people have been fooled? Did all of those girls lack spiritual discernment? Were they all gullible? Perhaps, but if you change the names and the faces, you'll discover that the above story has been repeated in many different churches. Perhaps it's happened to you.

It is amazing how the "wolf in sheep's clothing" operates. The honest and straight-shooting Christian has a difficult time imagining how anyone can lie, manipulate, and fornicate guiltlessly. We judge others by our standards only to find out that many people—even many professing Christians—don't have any standards at all. So how do you spot the wolf before he seduces you?

Probably the best information we have is found in Matthew 7:15-23, where Jesus lists the characteristics of the wolf. Study this passage. If you know what a wolf is and how he comes into the flock of God, you will be much more likely to spot and avoid him before he gets to you. ⑤

Signs of a Wolf

A wolf will attempt to lead you deeply into the forest with him so that he can make a meal of you. To spot the signs of a spiritual wolf before he comes your way and eats you up, study the following Bible references:

1. You must count on there being wolves in the flock (church) of God because Jesus predicted they would come (Matthew 7:15a; 24:11; Acts 20:29-30). If you expect to find them, chances are better that you won't be surprised by one.

2. Wolves come dressed like sheep (Matthew 7:15a). That means they will look like any other Christian, and usually can't be identified by their outward dress.

3. Wolves look good on the outside, but inwardly are ravenous (Matthew 7:15b). Generally, every wolf will let his hair down at some point. Listen carefully and cautiously to anyone out of whose mouth comes statements that are inconsistent with biblical Christianity.

4. Wolves may even say all the right words. True belief is seen not just in what we say, but in what we do (Matthew 7:21). Not everyone who professes to be a Christian is one.

5. Wolves sometimes will perform impressive spiritual acts. But even effective ministries aren't evidence of a person's faith in God if his deeds are lawless (Matthew 7:22-23; 24:24).

6. Wolves will secretly introduce destructive heresies among the brethren, often denying the Lord Jesus (2 Peter 2:1-2). This undermining of beliefs will always be done secretly, usually one-on-one, so that no one else will know what the wolves are really doing.

7. Wolves attempt to sway people into immorality. They will justify sexual involvement, and "many will follow their sensuality" (2 Peter 2:1-2; 1 Timothy 4:2).

8. Wolves must be spotted by their bad fruit or actions (Matthew 7:16-20), not their outward appearance. Look at their deeds and if the deeds are bad, you should be aware that you may be dealing with wolves instead of sheep. 👀

What Does It Mean?

A box of candy means friendship.
A bunch of flowers means love.
But a diamond ring means business.

Six Lines to Watch Out For
(For Girls Only)

How gullible are you? Do you know when a guy's just giving you a line? Lines are what you put hooks on; they are what you use to catch fish. Some guys use lines to get girls into bed.

Now it's totally possible that a guy may use a line without realizing that what he's saying is a line. But instinctively, when a boy is trying to talk a girl into doing more than she wants to do sexually, he comes up with certain statements to break down her resistance.

Here are what I call "the top six":

1 "I want to marry you." *Now that doesn't sound too threatening, does it? Yet I see this as the most dangerous line of all. When a guy begins to talk marriage to a girl, he's talking about the rest of their lives. It is so much easier for a girl to give in sexually if she thinks the relationship is going to go on for a lifetime.*

But remember, there is never any guarantee that you will get married—and a guy who starts talking about marriage early in a relationship is probably not thinking about marriage. He's probably thinking about deeper sexual involvement. It is inappropriate for a guy to talk about marriage until the relationship is really ready.

How can you know if it's too soon? If you're sixteen—or even seventeen—it's way too soon. If you're both in your twenties, but you know it will be a few years before you can get married, it's still too soon. The more permanent you think the relationship will be, the more likely that you'll destroy it with premature sexual involvement.

2 "I love you." Again, these words sound pretty harmless, but they can be deadly. When I was dating and really liked a girl, I found it difficult to say those magic words. I knew they went with a commitment I wasn't yet ready to give.

When a relationship has developed over a period of time, and suddenly your guy announces that he really "loves you," your feelings may soar out of control. This is what you have been waiting for—a commitment of undying love. But remember, those are only words. They may or may not represent how he feels today. Will he still love you tomorrow? Maybe not.

I know a girl who became pregnant. As soon as her boyfriend realized she was going to have a baby, he dumped her. Five months after she had had the baby, he came back. He would say, "I love you," but then sleep with other girls.

This girl came to me and asked, "Do you think he really loves me?" Even though he was treating her like dirt, she tended to believe his love line. She wanted to believe it. I told her, "Ignore what he says. Look at what he does. Does he behave like he really loves you?" Of course, the answer to that was No!

If you listen only to a guy's words, you may be fooled. Watch his behavior as well. One of the best ways to judge a guy's true intentions is to look at the way he lives his life. If he backs up his words with actions, it's much more likely that he is telling you the truth. But be careful! That still isn't any reason to have sex with him before marriage.

3 "If you really loved me, you would." *This line is a little more to the point. It is designed to bring out a girl's sense of guilt. It says, in effect, "You say you love me, but I don't know if I can believe you because you won't go to bed with me. If you really loved me, you wouldn't hurt me by withholding your love [sex] from me." The girl then feels she has to prove her love. She is being made to feel selfish if she doesn't give in.*

First, remember that love and sex are not the same thing. You can show your love very tangibly without doing anything sexual with your loved one. Love—especially before marriage—does not need or require sex to make it real.

Second, realize that he's manipulating you through fear. Ultimately he's saying, "If you don't love me enough to show it sexually, I'll just have to find someone who will." This works only if you fear losing him. But if that's what he's saying, you should quickly let him have his freedom.

Third, realize that any boy who tries to break down your God-given sense of right and wrong is not really interested in what is best for you. He's not worried about your loss of virginity, the fact that you could get pregnant, or any other consequences of premarital intimacy. He is thinking about how good it will feel for himself. Period.

The logical answer to this line is, "If you really love me, you won't ask me to violate myself like that." Lay it back on him. If you lose him, as hard as it may be for you to believe, you're better off.

4 "I love Jesus, and you love Jesus—let's love him together." *This line can be very subtle. It may not even be said. It may just be communicated through affection that comes after spiritual activities.*

When you are involved in spiritually and emotionally charged activities like witnessing, worshipping, or serious Bible study, you will discover deeper feelings for the Lord. If a member of the opposite sex shares those experiences with you, it is easy to transfer the affection you feel for the Lord to that person sitting next to you. When I was in high school and participating in ministry trips to Mexico, there were many romances that developed beyond what they should have in the back of our church bus. Don't allow yourself to be seduced by a mixture of spirituality and carnality. Believe it or not, the emotional highs from both can feel very similar.

5 "We've already done so much; what difference does it make?" *This is another line that attempts to work a girl's guilt level. What it really means is, "Hey, you've already lowered your standards with me. You can't tell me that your standards are high because I know differently. If you've gone this far, you should be willing to go all the way."*

Remember two wrongs don't make something right. If you have gone further than you should, what you need to do is break off the relationship completely for a while. The pressure to escalate your sexual involvement will be too great on you.

Don't let guilt for your past behavior cause you to let down your standards any further. When you hear this line, you know that it is a warning that you have gone too far. You need to turn away from your current involvement.

6

"We're already married in God's sight anyway." *This line usually takes place after a guy has talked long and heavy about marriage. He may even get you involved in some kind of private marriage ceremony in which you commit yourselves to each other and begin to feel you are truly "married in God's sight."*

The problem is that this really isn't a commitment. It's not legal, it's not moral, there are no earthly witnesses (the angels don't qualify), and it's done behind everyone's back. Your parents have no idea you've made such a commitment, because they'd be horrified if they did (Right?). And it violates everything God says about marriage in the Bible.

What it is is a great excuse for enjoying the benefits of being married—namely, sexual intercourse. Don't let any such "commitment" make you believe it's okay to have sex. A pseudo ceremony with no witnesses is really just an excuse to feed the flesh. If you let yourself be talked into something like that, you will only fool yourself.

A single guy once told me he knew a "Christian" couple who had done this. Although they were not married legally, they slept together because they said they were married in God's eyes. They attended a large church of several thousand people where no one knew who they were or what they were doing.

My question to him was, "What group do they belong to when they go to church? Do they go to the married group, or to the singles' group?" He admitted they went to the singles' group.

"Isn't that interesting?" I pointed out to him. "They claim they are married 'in God's eyes,' yet they still go to the singles' group. Even they know they're only kidding themselves."

Most often we use lines on others. But sometimes we use them on ourselves so we will have an excuse to live the way we want. I am reminded of the theme of the book of Judges. As the people of God kept falling into the same sins, we're told that "every man did what was right in his own eyes" (Judges 17:6). That's the key to ungodly living. If you want to blow your Christian life, just do what you think is right; don't consult God's Word. But, of course, God has a better way.

BE A MAN!

GET CONFIDENT!

Does your brain turn into Jell-O
every time a girl looks at you?
Does your stomach do a belly-flop
if a girl actually smiles in your direction?
If so, you need **Confidence,**
the cologne that will make a man out of you.

There has never been an after-shave like this.
Just splash it on your face and suddenly
you'll start acting like the man you want to be.
Nothing can stop you when you have
real **Confidence.**
Girls will be so impressed by you
that they'll fight for your attention.
How have you survived so long without:

Confidence

Cologne & After-shave Lotion

Available Everywhere
(we can talk people into letting us sell it)

Thoughts about Love

"In love there is always one who kisses and one who offers the cheek." —French Proverb

"Money cannot buy love, but it makes shopping for it a lot easier."
—Anonymous

"Love is like an hourglass, with the heart filling up as the brain empties."
—Jules Renard

"The love that lasts the longest is the love that is never returned."
—W. Somerset Maugham

"Love is a hole in the heart."
—Ben Hecht

Are You Gullible?

*T*hey say that you can fool all of the people some of the time, some of the people all of the time, but you can't fool all of the people all of the time. Although few people are completely gullible, researchers believe that some are a lot more gullible than others. A "highly persuadable person" is the kind of person who will buy the Brooklyn Bridge, if the price is right. Just about anyone can pull the wool over such a person's eyes. Some people, on the other hand, have the ability to spot phonies and rip-off artists a mile away. Which type of person are you?

Intelligence seems to have very little to do with how gullible you are. An Einstein can be duped as easily as a dim-witted person. The person who firmly believes he can't be hustled is often an easier mark than one who thinks he's a pushover. In fact, cons often find it easy to rip off other cons. Our own opinion of how susceptible we are to being conned seems to have little relation to reality.

While P. T. Barnum may have been right when he said that there is a sucker born every minute, it also seems true that how you are raised will have a lot to do with your "sucker-ability." Highly susceptible people often fear being around others and have feelings of inadequacy. They tend to like things well organized, and usually are passive, waiting for others to lead them. Because they don't always trust their own judgment, they're more willing to listen to, and accept, the arguments of others.

Gullible people may have strong feelings, but they tend not to show them very often. They may live in a world of elaborate daydreams in which they are more in control. Because they tend toward idealistic attitudes, they really want to believe the lines that they are given.

In contrast, people who are hard to deceive usually have strong opinions that they won't give up without a fight. They have enough confidence in their own beliefs, judgments, and opinions to make it difficult to hook them with a line.

Hard-to-deceive people tend to be at ease with others and mix easily with strangers. They usually feel good about themselves and take a direct approach to life. They dislike opposition but are still aggressive and drive hard. They can become strong leaders, or become the guys who make suckers out of the rest of us.

Not the Only Pebble

"If you want to win her hand
Let the maiden understand
That she's not the only pebble
    on the beach."

—Harry Braisted

Games We Play for Love

*P*eople involved in romantic love play games. Not necessarily because games are fun, but because games serve an end. Most of us learn this at a young age when we innocently show interest in someone, only to be rejected by them. We act less interested, and suddenly we have found a technique that works better: when I play that I am not interested in you (though I really am), I make myself harder to get—and suddenly I discover *you* want *me*. I have obtained your interest without risking my pride.

Love's games are learned by trial and error. Every error we make causes us to look for new ways of overcoming our mistakes. Every success we have encourages us that certain methods tend to work better with the opposite sex.

Pretty soon, learning how to play the game well becomes more important than who we're playing it with. The partners may change, but the important thing is to win. For guys, winning may mean "scoring" sexually. For girls, it may mean snagging a boyfriend to show off to their friends. The object of the game is no longer a relationship with someone—it is just winning something from them.

A guy may desire to build his "reputation" almost like a gunfighter puts notches on his gun. He wants to be thought of by his peers as a Don Juan, a Casanova, a real man, a stud. He looks forward to sharing (and perhaps expanding) his exploits during locker-room conversations. He likes to be able to brag with the boys about how "good" he is.

Girls generally don't brag about their sexual prowess. They usually want to be thought of as attractive and desirable. They want to be popular and sought after. To go out with many of the more popular jocks, or one of the cool set, can be a real sign that a girl is "with it."

This is the way of the game for many young people. Eventually, most teens feel that they will settle down with one person when the "right one comes along." But if you've been playing games, getting what you can get when you can get it, how do you stop? How can you become real with someone when you have been artificial for so long?

But if you've been playing games, getting what you can get when you can get it, how do you stop?

Sure, if you are really moved by someone, you'll find ways to honestly reveal yourself. But if you've been masking your true self for a long time because of your fear of being hurt, it will be very difficult.

There is a better way.

Died of a Broken Heart

Theodora Cooper was forbidden to marry her cousin, poet William Cowper, when they were youngsters. When she died sixty-eight years later, her tombstone proclaimed that she had died of a broken heart.

The Higher Road

*T*rue love, as opposed to romantic love, is a willingness to be real because you know that game-playing keeps relationships on a childish level. True love is being willing to suffer pain because you want to grow up. Growing up requires pain.

True love means risking rejection a few times in order to find a person with whom you can have a stable, lifelong relationship. It means knowing that the only way to have such a relationship is to make certain that you don't play games.

You can learn what true love is all about only by loving. All of us are born with the capacity to love. This can be seen in the way we are instantly drawn to our parents—especially our mothers—in a close bond while we are still babies. But our capacity for love is fragile. If our parents or other loved ones don't return our affection, we soon find it more difficult to give love.

No matter how you may have been rejected in the past, it is important to know that God loves you. He was rejected by us, yet he came to give to us and make us lovable. It is his love that allows us to love and moves us to reach out to others.

When you choose to love, as God loves, without games or pretenses, you will end up in a mature love relationship. If you don't start loving honestly, you can never hope to get honest love in return. You must give what you want to receive. In Jesus, you can find the love and the identity we all secretly long for. ♡

Quiz

Jealousy: The Mark of Cain

Shakespeare called jealousy "the green-eyed monster." Some have called it the "mark of Cain," after the biblical Cain who killed his brother Abel because he was jealous of him.

Most of us have no trouble recognizing the symptoms of jealousy in others. If we're honest, we can usually spot the monster lurking in ourselves. When we are hurt because our boyfriend or girlfriend wants to spend time with someone else, it is a sign that jealousy is rearing its ugly head.

Jealousy kills relationships. If we are not willing to let someone go, sooner or later we will lose them anyway. When we try to exercise too much control over the freedom someone else has, we soon discover that jealousy brings on the very thing we fear most. It repels our lover and pushes him or her into the arms of someone who is more understanding.

Do certain types of people tend to become jealous more than others? Yes. Certain types of experiences tend to make us more susceptible to jealous feelings.

Take the following quiz and see if you have experienced things that make it easier for you to be a jealous suitor. Answer yes or no to each question.

1. **When you go somewhere with your girlfriend or boyfriend, do you think he or she should be at your side all night?**

2. **Do you ever think you're not much fun to be with?**

3. **Would anyone say that you're "too conscientious?"**

4. **Is it difficult for you to relax, even when you're tired?**

5. **Did (or does) your parents' marriage have problems?**

6. **Do you think that you should be the dominant partner in any relationship?**

7. Does it bother you that others have more material things than you do?

8. Do you think some of your teachers criticize you more than others in your classes?

9. Were you pampered as a child? Answer this truthfully!

10. When you are criticized, do you explode in anger, or get extremely depressed?

11. Do you give in easily when people try to change your opinion?

12. Are you timid, or too polite, with people you can't stand?

13. When you meet someone who is more attractive and intelligent than you are, do you secretly want to see them get "cut down to size"?

14. Has anyone in your immediate family experienced a marriage breakup?

15. Do you often feel lonely?

16. Do you often feel guilty for your behavior?

17. Do you have trouble with alcohol?

If you have more "yes" than "no" answers, you may have tendencies to be jealous. You may not feel very secure in your own identity. Much of this may come from the way your parents treat you or treat each other. Jealous people often are trying to prove to themselves that they really are worthwhile.

If you scored high on this quiz, it does not mean that you are doomed to be a jealous person. It just means that you tend to lean in that direction. What can you do about it? Read on.

Overcoming the Green-Eyed Monster

*J*ealousy and envy are close companions. It is difficult to tell one from the other. If you think that you are not getting all that you deserve, and wish you were in someone else's shoes because he's getting what you would like to have, you're envious.

Jealousy, on the other hand, is fear of being replaced by someone else. You secretly wonder when the person you love will turn you in for a new model. You believe that you aren't as "together" as other people, so you don't want to give your boyfriend or girlfriend a long leash for fear that he or she will find someone better.

The Bible says that "love . . . is not jealous [or envious]" (1 Corinthians 13:4b). How can we not be jealous (or envious)? It's really rather simple. God has injected his agape love into us. When we invite Christ to come and live in our lives, we receive his Spirit too. Because God's agape love is already within us, all we have to do is let his Spirit have free reign, and it will come out.

At the core of jealousy and envy is a feeling of insecurity. But when God accepts us into his family, he declares that we have tremendous value. If he sent his Son to die on the cross for us, we must certainly be of great worth to him. He cares what happens to us and promises that if we put him first, all of our needs will be met (Matthew 6:33). He also promises that everything will work out for the best if we are continually letting him "shape" us into his image (Romans 8:28-29).

Because God accepts us, we can learn to accept ourselves. Certainly, he does not like our sin, nor does he put a rubber stamp of approval on it. But he accepts us as we are, knowing that we must be changed for our own benefit. He is willing to give us the time we need to work on those changes.

The Bible actually says that God is a jealous God. But God is jealous in a righteous way. He knows that if we "play the harlot after other gods" (Judges 2:17), as he puts it, we will destroy ourselves. He is jealous for our good, not because he is insecure in his position as God. He knows we need him. If God is able to use his jealousy to serve righteous purposes, we must also be able to turn our jealous feelings into acts of righteousness.

Loving someone enough to give them the freedom to turn away from you, just like God does, is a choice you can make. You can decide to let God's agape love take control of your heart so that you transcend your normal fear of being rejected. God wants you to give him those feelings of insecurity (1 Peter 5:7; Philippians 4:6-7).

Lord, what do you want? should be the question you continually ask. When you worry more about pleasing God, you will be amazed at how little time you have left to worry about meeting your own needs.

*S*pirit-Led Roma

five

e

Put the Spirit Back into Your Love Life

*I*f something is romantic, isn't it also sinful and out of control? It certainly can be, but I think it is possible to be romantic and still be under the power and control of the Holy Spirit.

Remember that God is the one who made us with the capability for romantic feelings. He is the one who designed our bodies with all of their intriguing responses to sexual stimuli. God doesn't have anything against sex, considering that he invented it. He just wants it to be exercised in the framework of marriage.

If you go to an inventor and ask for his opinion on something he designed, you have to believe that he is the best judge of how to work that invention. In the same way, everything that God has created has a right and best use. It also has a wrong use. God knows best how we are to use romantic sex.

Yes, sex is exciting outside of marriage; if it weren't, no one would be tempted to fool around. But its capacity to bring pleasure to a couple within a marriage relationship surpasses any pleasures obtained outside of marriage.

When a person consistently does what is wrong, he dulls his sense of right and wrong and develops a jaded taste. Soon only immorality, or perverted sex, can give him the highs he craves. Romance is degraded by becoming an endless search for higher highs.

When a person consistently does what is wrong, he dulls his sense of right and wrong and develops a jaded taste.

But when God's Spirit controls your love life, you feel a whole new kind of excitement. The chemistry God has built into your body is unleashed in a monogamous direction. Your senses begin to respond in the way that God designed, in the way they function best.

God can do wonderful things in your love life!

Changed by Love

"One is changed by what one loves, sometimes to the point of losing one's entire identity."
—Joseph Brodsky

Training Your Senses

Jerry Hatfield always systematically shakes out his leg and arm muscles before a marathon race. It is a pre-race ritual he follows religiously to help his superbly trained body relax. He has spent many hours conditioning his body and mind in order to be a winner in these long runs.

The apostle Paul uses athletic training as an illustration in 1 Corinthians 9:25, 27. He says, "And everyone who competes in the games exercises self-control in all things. . . . I buffet [or discipline] my body and make it my slave, lest possibly, after I have preached to others, I myself should be disqualified." God wants you to train your senses for marriage in the same way you would train your body for a race.

Does this idea sound new to you? The following Bible-based suggestions may help you better understand how to condition yourself.

1. Train your senses to discern the difference between good and evil through practice and through intake of God's Word. *Hebrews 5:14 says, "But solid food [the Word of God through the Spirit] is for the mature, who because of practice have their senses trained to discern good and evil."*

You're probably thinking, "What can be so hard about telling the difference between good and evil? That should be pretty simple." But evil can mask itself as good so that you can be fooled. Evil isn't always gross and obvious; sometimes it is beautiful and seductive.

But how do you practice training your senses? I believe this passage is saying that as you apply the Word of God to your life on a regular basis, your senses will learn to discern between the good and bad choices you have to make daily. The practice involves staying in God's Word.

2. Train your senses through intake of God's Word. *Hebrews 4:12 and 13 says, "For the word of God is living and active and sharper than any two-edged sword, and piercing as far as the division of soul and spirit, of both joints and marrow, and able to judge the thoughts and intentions of the heart. And there is no creature hidden from His sight, but all things are open and laid bare to the eyes of Him with whom we have to do."*

God knows your heart better than you do. His Word is designed to slice deep within your heart to convict and reprove you in areas where you need to grow. His Word is the unchanging standard by which you can measure all activities and input. Our judgment has a tendency to change, based upon what we may be feeling or desiring at any given moment. God's Word remains solid and sure.

Second Timothy 3:16 tells us, *"All Scripture is inspired by God and profitable for teaching, for reproof, for correction, for training in righteousness."* Allow your thoughts and actions to be exposed to his Word on a regular basis and it will train your senses.

3. *Expose yourself only to what is good. Romans 16:19 says, "I want you to be wise in what is good, and innocent in what is evil." Make a practice of exposing yourself to what is good. Work at spending time in church, at Bible studies, spending time in prayer, and in general doing those activities that will develop your sense of what is right and good.*

"Good" doesn't just happen; it has to be developed. The more you expose yourself to it, the more you will enjoy it.

4. *Do not expose yourself to evil. In 1 Corinthians 14:20 we read, "Brethren, do not be children in your thinking; yet in evil be babes." While we are encouraged to experience good, we are told to stay away from what is evil.*

There are times you will have to force yourself to turn off a video, change channels on the television set, turn off the radio, or walk out of a movie theater. If you are exposing your senses to graphically detailed images of evil that may stick in your brain, put your foot down. Tell yourself you simply will not let garbage in through your eyes and ears. Your mind doesn't have a very effective erase button for strong images.

5. Learn to see all graphic depictions of sex in movies, videos, on television, and in books as the prostitution of sex. *Proverbs 2 talks about listening to the wisdom of God so that you can be delivered from the "strange woman" (2:16). "Strange sex" is any sexual involvement with a member of the opposite sex who is not your spouse.*

The apostle Paul tells us to "flee immorality" (1 Corinthians 6:18). Jesus made it plain that immoral thoughts were equal to immoral actions. "You have heard that it was said, 'You shall not commit adultery'; but I say to you, that everyone who looks on a woman to lust for her has committed adultery with her already in his heart" (Matthew 5:27-28). Therefore, you should run from any dramatization of immorality.

6. Learn to stand alone. *Daniel 1:8 says, "But Daniel made up his mind that he would not defile himself with the king's choice food or with the wine which he drank; so he sought permission from the commander of the officials that he might not defile himself." Learn to stand alone like Daniel.*

If all of your friends—even your Christian friends—are attending a beer party, for instance, you should be willing to stand alone and say, "I'm sorry. Because of my relationship with Jesus Christ, I have chosen not to expose myself to certain things, and this is one of them."

7. Train yourself to be pure. *Titus 1:15 says, "To the pure, all things are pure; but to those who are defiled and unbelieving, nothing is pure, but both their mind and their conscience are defiled."*

Once you've developed a pure attitude toward romance, you will have a difficult time responding to unrighteousness. Obscene jokes won't be funny to you. Many of the television situation comedies which are filled with sexual innuendoes will turn you off. You will want to avoid any music (secular or Christian) that causes your mind to wander from a deep relationship with Christ.

8. Train yourself to be consistent in righteousness. *Consistency in righteousness comes through walking in the Spirit. "But I say, walk by the Spirit, and you will not carry out the desire of the flesh. For the flesh sets its desire against the Spirit, and the Spirit against the flesh; for these are in opposition to one another, so that you may not do the things that you please" (Galatians 5:16-17, emphasis added).*

Walking in the Spirit involves setting your mind on the things of the Spirit (see also Romans 8:5) and not the flesh. Consistency in righteousness is achieved first in the mind. The body will do what it is supposed to do if your mind is under the control of the Spirit. ♡

The Trust Factor

Blondin, a famous nineteenth-century French high wire walker, set up a wire across Niagara Falls. Huge crowds formed to watch him cross back and forth. Then he asked the audience if they believed he could take a man across to the other side. Everyone thought he had the ability to do so. But no one wanted to get on his back. Finally, his manager climbed on, and Blondin carried him across the river.

We're a little like that crowd. We believe God can do some marvelous things, but we have no intention of climbing on board to find out for certain. We're not sure he will do it for *us*.

How much do you trust God? How would you measure it? Read the following statements to see how many of them you can answer yes to. Try to be truthful. If you find it difficult or impossible to agree with any statement, admit it honestly to yourself so that you will have a better idea of the areas where you need help.

1. "I trust God enough to live for him; I have dedicated my life to him."
2. "I trust God enough to die for him."
3. "I trust him enough to let him choose who I am going to marry."
4. "I trust God enough to let him choose what I will do when I get out of school."
5. "I trust God with my talents; if he wants to use them, great. But if he doesn't want to use them, that's OK."
6. "Although I might find it difficult, if God wants me to serve him in a foreign country, I will go."
7. "I trust God with my sex life; I'm willing to wait until I'm married."
8. "I trust God enough to listen to what he has to say through my parents."
9. "I trust him enough that if he says I need to break off a relationship with someone, I will do it."
10. "I trust God enough to wait on him, and not dash off to run my own life."

Learning to trust God fully takes time. Just remember that he sent his Son to die in your place. He loves you as much as his own Son—more than you love yourself! So trusting him makes a lot of sense.

Once you experience God's trustworthiness, you will be able to look at your love life from a completely different perspective. You'll want his involvement. You'll want his opinion about each person you date. You'll want his encouragement or discouragement to keep you on the path that leads to a healthy romantic relationship and perhaps a successful future marriage.

"Faith" Bible Study

1. Why is it impossible to please God without faith? (See Hebrews 11:6.)

2. Why does a person have to acknowledge God's existence in order to come to him? (Read Hebrews 11:6 again.)

3. How is faith defined in Hebrews 11:1? Analyze the definition given.

4. How did God allow Abraham's faith to make him righteous? (See Romans 4:5.)

5. Is faith real if it does not produce any good deeds? (See James 2:14-26.)

Knowing God's Peace

When I was in college, an older friend named Randy came into the cafeteria and announced he was engaged. I pulled him aside and asked, "Randy, Debby's really cute, but how can you be certain she's the one? You've dated a lot of different girls. How can you know for certain God is really in this?"

"Peace, John. That's how I know," Randy replied. He had me read Colossians 3:15, which says, "And let the peace of Christ rule [or stand guard] in your hearts."

"This is the first girl with whom I've ever had that peace," he continued. "Don't get married unless you have that peace."

I remember thinking, "That's pretty simplistic." But Randy's words stayed with me for the rest of my dating years.

Your relationship with the Lord should be close enough so you will have a definite feeling of "being out of his will," a lack of peace, when you are about to make a poor choice. Certainly, you can make mistakes here. If you had too much pizza the night before, your heartburn could conceivably be read as something more than it is. But we all know when our relationship with a close friend is not quite right. When you feel that way with God, you should back off and wait for his peace.

Make a long-term commitment to let the peace of Christ rule in every situation you encounter. Make it a habit to let the peace of Christ rule in your romantic life. You won't be sorry if you do.

Who Gets the Girl?

A plague in Weitensfeld, Austria, wiped out the entire town, except for one girl and three young men. The men promptly had a foot race to determine who would get the girl. That race is restaged each year.

Losing to Win

"The way to love anything
is to realize that it might be lost."
—G. K. Chesterton

True Love Often Has to Say Good-Bye

I thought the sinking feeling I had in the pit of my stomach would never go away. Diane was the most beautiful girl I had ever dated. She had a slim, but shapely figure, a superb way of dressing, and a lovable personality. She had even become a Christian a few months back. Yet, her Christianity was not yet at the maturity level I needed in a wife. I knew that God was telling me to say good-bye.

Actually, I had known for some time.

Late one night while we were sitting on a curb together in front of her house, an overwhelming thought, *She's not the one,* had rolled over me. I remember saying to myself, *Whoa! This must be my imagination. Surely the Lord can't be speaking to me this way.* But I could not shake that lack of peace. It lasted for months.

Letting go of Diane was one of the hardest things I ever had to do. Nevertheless, I didn't want to continue dating her, no matter how perfect she was in other ways, if she was not the girl God wanted for me. So I let go, and the relationship ended.

Six long years later I was steadily dating a special girl who was everything that Diane had been, but was also a turned-on Christian. Only once again, I had that feeling that it was time to break off the relationship. Could it be that I was never going to get married? If I said good-bye again, I might remain single for life! I had waited too long to find someone as perfect as Susie. Still, I knew that our relationship was over until God said otherwise.

We both cried. My decision was not easy for either of us. But then, before I left, Susie gave me a collage she had been working on. She had taken the classified ad section of the newspaper and glued several interesting quotes to it. They said exactly what I was

feeling. How could she have known in advance what I was feeling?

When I saw Susie at church the next day, I just wanted to be with her. I asked her if she would sit with me during the second service even though she had already sat through the first service by herself. She agreed. Then we went over to her house and spent some more time together. Without a doubt, I now felt peace. So much so that the following Thursday I asked her to marry me, and by the end of the year, we were married.

If you really love the Lord, you will be willing to trust him enough to say "good-bye" to someone if he tells you it's necessary. As one who's had to do it twice, I'll admit that it's not easy. But God is the only one who really knows what's best for you.

If you depend upon your own feelings, you'll probably end up making a serious mistake. There are things that you can't know about the future. You don't know how someone will change.

When I entered my early twenties, I realized that although I was attracted toward outgoing girls, I really was happier around quieter girls. I had changed as I had grown older, and if I had gotten married early, I would have married the wrong type of girl.

Determine to let God put his stamp of approval on anyone you are interested in. You will save yourself a lot of heartache in the long run.

Can You Spot the Ringers?

Take a good look at the three men above and choose which one you think will be the best husband.

If you chose number one, you just selected a future trash collector and geek.

If you picked number three, you selected a future bum. Looks can certainly be deceiving. How can you tell for sure if your guy is the man of your dreams . . . or a refugee from your night-mares? Simple! Just use our top-secret, hand-held **RINGER SPOTTER**!

There has never been a better way to determine anyone's hidden personality than with this brand new high-tech invention. The **RINGER SPOTTER** was developed by a computer expert to help his daughter avoid weirdos. Now you too can benefit from using this unusual device.

Just send $300 cash[1] to the address given below and we'll rush this invention to you. Only the first 200 to send in their cash will be eligible for this great price, so hurry. (This offer is void where prohibited by law[2].)

TOP-SECRET OFFER
33 Get-It-Quick Street
Silicon Valley, California

The Fine Print
[1] We have to have cash so there won't be any record of the transaction.
[2] But don't worry, the law has to catch us before they can prohibit us.

Tips to Help You Stay Out of Fantasyland

Quality Loving

"Let grace and goodness be the principal loadstone of thy affections. For love which hath ends, will have an end; whereas that which is founded on true virtue, will always continue."
—John Dryden

"One of the deep secrets of life is that all that is really worth the doing is what we do for others."
—Lewis Carroll

"To love is good, too: love being difficult. For one human being to love another: that is perhaps the most difficult of all our tasks, the ultimate, the last test and proof, the work for which all other work is but preparation."
—Rainer Maria Rilke

1. *Tell yourself the truth.* The Bible pulls no punches. It explains human nature like it is. It makes it plain that people are basically wicked. Just because somebody is a Christian doesn't mean that he doesn't still have a sinful nature to deal with.

2. *Seek wise counsel.* Proverbs 11:14 tells us that there is much wisdom in many counselors. Seeking an outside opinion from people who are experienced in life is very important in order to see things clearly. When you seek counsel, look for people who have made

a success of their lives and marriages, and who follow the Word of God. If a person has no respect for the Bible, he'll probably give you advice that is contradictory to it. And that you don't need.

3. Seek the counsel of your parents. Usually they want what is best for you. Many teenagers say that because their parents are not Christians, they don't want to ask for their advice. Don't write off your parents if they are unbelievers. God may speak to you through unbelieving parents, even after you are old enough to leave home. If your parents

know that you value and respect their opinions, the chances are good that you'll get the best possible advice from them.

4. Learn to wait on the Lord. This is probably one of the most difficult things for most of us to do. When we want something, we want it *now*. So we rush out to get it, only to discover when we look more closely that there is something wrong with what we

wanted. Being patient is the secret to getting almost everything that is of any value.

Wait for God to show you what he wants you to do, as well as when and how to do it. If God wants you to pursue a relationship, he is completely capable of pushing you ahead. What happens is that you become afraid if you don't move fast enough, you'll lose the one you're interested in. What if he or she finds someone else while you're busy praying about them? If that happens, God never meant that relationship to be. Taking time and depending on the Lord to speak never hurt any child of God.

5. *Pray for guidance.* Ask God for clear direction. When you pray, don't forget to listen. You'll probably be surprised at the things he'll put in your head. Usually you'll know they are his thoughts because they won't line up with what you would normally do. Even then, take your time and seek a confirmation of his will in your life.

6. *Seek God's will through his Word.* This is important. Remember that God will never contradict himself by telling you to do something that his Word expressly tells you not to do, or vice versa.

For example, if you think you feel

God telling you to marry a non-believer, you can know that God isn't the one speaking. The Bible clearly teaches that we are not to be "unequally yoked," or married to unbelievers (2 Corinthians 6:14; 1 Corinthians 7:39).

This is why it is extremely important to spend time getting to know God's Word. It will keep you from giving your heart and life to people who are not walking in God's ways. It will reveal to you the "thoughts and intentions of the heart" (Hebrews 4:12-13).

six

KeepingRomance

When the Honeymoon Is Over

Jamie Kirk sat on the edge of the motel bed and burst into tears. Although it had been several minutes since Jack had slammed the door and gone for a walk, she could still feel its vibration in her tired head.

The Kirks were still on their honeymoon, and already she and Jack had had heated words. She had hoped that all of their frequent courtship disagreements would end once they got married. But this one was worse than any they had had before marriage. And the argument was so silly. It had started when she had asked him to pick up his underwear off the motel room floor.

Alive

We like to think that feelings of love never end. After all, isn't that what storybook romances are made of? Unending love? But the reality is that there will come a day, after the knot is tied, when you will wonder if you made a mistake.

For my wife, it was about two months after we were married. We had our first real argument on a Sunday afternoon right before evening church. Because I was a youth pastor, and had to leave for church right away, I told her, "Look, I don't want us to go with this tension between us. I have to be there because of my position, so why don't you stay home? We'll talk this out when I get back."

She told me later that she was devastated. She sat down on the bed and cried. The argument was so unlike what we had experienced earlier in our relationship that she wondered if this was the beginning of the end. And she couldn't believe that I had actually gone to church without her.

The cold hard reality of married life was starting to set in. This marriage was not going to be perfect. It would have its share of problems. She and I would just have to work through them. The honeymoon was over, but the work of building our marriage was just beginning.

Most of us marry an illusion. Sooner or later, however, all illusions come to an end, and we have to start living in the real world where people get angry and forget to use their deodorant and don't clean up their own messes. How do you cope with this real world when you've been living in Fantasyland?

You cope by working to make your relationship as good as it can be. Every marriage, no matter how ideal it may seem, will take work. It must be worked on if it is going to grow. But remember, your marriage will certainly be worth all that you put into it.

After all the years my wife and I have been married, I can tell you that our hard work has been worthwhile. Sure, there have been difficult moments, like that first real argument. But the good so overwhelms any bad that I can highly recommend marriage as one of God's most exciting and creative ideas. ♡

Unquenchable Love

"Many waters cannot quench love,
Nor will rivers overflow it;
If a man were to give all the riches
  of his house for love
It would be utterly despised."
—Solomon (Song of Solomon 8:7)

What Is Romanticism?

It is a form of literature consisting of a little prose, a lot of poetry, but mostly just love letters.

Giving Up on Love

My telephone rang. A woman was calling to give me the call letters of her southern California radio station. She informed me we'd be on the air in about two minutes.

I enjoy doing radio interviews. This one was to discuss my campus magazine, *Marry.* Up to this point, all of my interviews had been with Christian stations.

The interview did not begin well. Right in the middle of my first answer, the brash DJ said to me, "Hey, can you just leave God out of this? I'm sure that there are a lot of people in our radio audience who would be inter-

ested in your book if you just left God out of this." It took me a second to recover. Then I realized I was being interviewed by a secular station.

What the radio DJ couldn't understand is that the absence of God is the problem in too many marriages. People choose—either on purpose or accidentally—to leave God out of their married lives. The result is that two people end up living together in mutual manipulation, taking whatever they can from their spouse until each gets tired of being used.

The early morning interview continued with a traffic report, and then a few call-ins from listeners. The DJ asked one of the callers, "Tell me, Bob, what do you think about marriage?"

"Well, don't get me wrong, but I don't believe in it anymore," said Bob. "I've been married twice, and I think that it's best for a guy and a girl each to have their own lives. My girlfriend and I each have our own apartments. That's the only way to go."

Bob's arrangement may sound great to a lot of people, especially those who have had a divorce or two: Have a relationship, but don't get married. But that doesn't mean, does it, that if the relationship breaks up, it will be any less traumatic? People are still people. They still hurt when someone leaves them for another.

The caller was burned out on marriage because his two hadn't worked. Why didn't they work? I'm convinced marriages often don't work because two self-centered people try to get the most out of their relationship with the least amount of "give."

When you don't have marriage, what do you have? A relationship of convenience without any commitment. If you have no real commitment, you don't have much of a relationship.

Living together, by its very nature, says, "I love you, but I don't trust you and I don't trust me. We may not feel this way tomorrow. Therefore, I don't want to be tied down to you because either you or I may want to have a new relationship with someone else the day after tomorrow."

When a couple gives up on marriage, they are really giving up on love. They're saying that their love is not strong enough to weather the test of time, and they do not trust it. I've seen people become bitter toward members of the opposite sex because they couldn't live successfully with them. What a shame that people give up on love!

Don't Shut It Out

"He that shuts love out,
in turn shall be shut out from love,
and on her threshold lie howling in outer darkness."
—Alfred, Lord Tennyson

"The great tragedy of life is not that men perish,
but that they cease to love."
—W. Somerset Maugham

ARE YOU WORTH

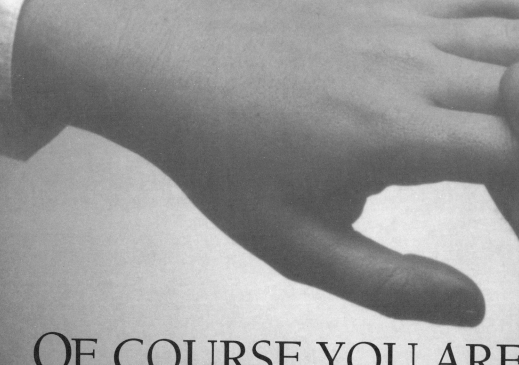

OF COURSE YOU ARE

But not just any diamond—only a decadently expensive diamond from Tippan

What's the difference between an ordinary diamond and a Decadent Diamond

You know he loves you if he is willing to pay our ridiculous prices. So why sett

for any other diamond when you can demand—and get—a Tippany?

A DIAMOND?

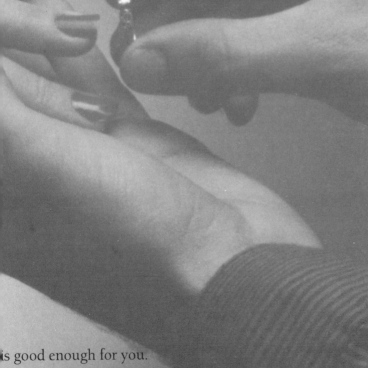

is good enough for you.

from Tippany? *Only the Cost!*

U$_n$u$_s$u$_a$l Customs

- In Borneo, the women of the Kalabit tribe propose marriage to the men, who are not allowed to refuse.

- Women of Gardena, in the Italian Tyrol, at one time wore tableware suspended from belts over their bridal gowns. This was to certify to their grooms that they had mastered the art of cooking.

- In the Shadozai tribe in Pakistan, a woman is permitted to wear trousers only once during her lifetime—on her wedding day.

- During a typical wedding ceremony in the Sulu tribe in the Philippines, the bride and groom are each carried on the shoulders of the guests.

- Women of the Nambas tribe of Malekula in the New Hebrides marry at the age of twelve and are required to put on heavy hair wigs, which they must wear night and day until their deaths.

- In the Kareng tribe of Guinea, young couples are permitted to marry against the wishes of their parents if they wear masks and use assumed names.

- In some rural parts of Yugoslavia, the mother of the bride must dance with each guest while balancing the wedding cake on her head.

Sacrificial Love

*I*n Charles Dickens' *A Tale of Two Cities,* Sydney Carton goes willingly to the French guillotine in the place of Charles Darnay. Both Carton and Darnay are in love with the same woman, Lucie Manette. But Carton knows that she cares more for Darnay than for him. To Carton, giving up his life for the sake of Lucie's happiness is "a far, far better thing [to] do, than I have ever done."

Dickens' story of sacrifice, unfortunately rare in real life, shows what agape love is all about. Agape love is a self-sacrificial love. When we love somebody with this kind of love, we are willing to do whatever is necessary for the good of the one we love. That may mean personal suffering, and it may even mean death. Jesus said, "Greater love has no one than this, that one lay down his life for his friends" (John 15:13).

The apostle Paul describes agape love's enduring quality in 1 Corinthians 13:7-8: Love "bears all things, believes all things, hopes all things, endures all things. Love never fails." All love that springs from how good someone makes you feel is shallow and sure to end. But agape love is much stronger and can continue even in the face of rejection.

You will never truly understand agape love until you have a relationship with Jesus Christ. No one has that ability to love within himself. It is only when we invite Jesus Christ to live within us that we gain the ability to live above our natural desires.

Our natural love desires are for self-fulfillment. We often think we are interested only in making our lovers happy, but if that happiness means they will spend their lives with someone else, we quickly realize we want our own happiness first. Only God loves unselfishly. We can love in that same way if we have him working within our conscious minds, energizing us.

Agape love often flowers in pressure environments. For instance, if you find yourself married to someone who does not want to follow the Lord as you do, you will need to love with agape love. I do not believe that God wants you to have to go through this.

But if you marry someone God didn't want you to marry, or if your Christian spouse should turn away from God, then you can apply this self-sacrificial love to the situation you are in.

Agape love doesn't give up. People who live by human standards give up all the time. That's why there are so many divorces. As a Christian, God has called you to a higher level of commitment.

So what is that commitment? Open your Bible to 1 Peter 2:21–3:7 and read the passage to discover for yourself. As you read, think about Christ's commitment to us, the commitment of spouses to each other, and the suffering that comes with that commitment.

Bible Study: Marriage and Suffering (1 Peter 2:21–3:7)

1. What does this passage say about suffering and its connection with marriage?

2. Is suffering always bad? (See 2:21.)

3. List the examples of Christ's suffering that are given: (See 2:23-24.)

4. What might suffering for your spouse accomplish? (See 3:1-7.)

5. Why is a wife to be in submission to her non-believing husband? (See 3:1.)

6. How is a Christian husband to treat his wife? (See 3:7.)

A Lifetime Marriage

Years ago, the divorce ratio among Christian couples who were involved in Bible study and prayer together was reputed to be one in every thousand marriages. That was a pretty impressive statistic. Unfortunately, far more Christians end up in divorce court today than they did when I heard that statistic. Part of the difference may be that believing couples don't pray and study the Word together. But I think the biggest problem is that we have accepted the world's mentality.

A worldly view says, "Hey, if this marriage doesn't work, I can always end it

107

and marry someone else." Christians who have adopted this view see marriage as a lifetime commitment only if it "works." If it ceases to work, there are many other fish in the sea.

The Word of God disagrees with this common view. Read 1 Corinthians 7:10-11: "But to the married I give instructions, not I, but the Lord, that the wife should not leave her husband (but if she does leave, let her remain unmarried, or else be reconciled to her husband), and that the husband should not send his wife away."

What is this Scripture saying?

1. *This passage is addressed to those who are married as Christians.* If you look at the context of the passage, you will notice that verses 12 through 16 are for those who are married to non-believers.

2. *Each half of the Christian couple is encouraged not to divorce the other partner.* The word "leave" here refers to "divorce," not just "separation." Because a person cannot legally remarry if he separates from his spouse, it is obvious that divorce is being talked about.

The only biblical ground for divorce

among two believers is infidelity (see Matthew 19:9). But that doesn't mean that infidelity on the part of your spouse demands that there be a divorce. In fact, the apostle Paul is discouraging divorce among Christians in 1 Corinthians 7:10.

I believe he's saying, "You are not to divorce your spouse if at all possible, but if you have to, because of gross immorality, then you have two choices: either stay unmarried, or reconcile with your former spouse. Remarriage is not an option."

3. *The Christian who divorces himself (or herself) from another Christian is not to remarry.* I believe the Lord is saying, "I've called you to remain single even if your spouse blows it." Does it really matter what the sinning spouse does? When you commit yourself to him or her for your entire life, you're promising, "there will be no one else but you."

Now you may say, "That's not fair! Suppose my spouse commits adultery and then leaves me for another person? Am I supposed to suffer just because he or she sinned?" My question then is, Does your spouse's sin justify you remarrying against the will of God?

The problem is one of commitment. If you are afraid you might get stuck later, do you really give your complete commitment? If you can't say, "It's you or no one at all," what you're saying is, "As long as our love lasts." And that makes your commitment no different than the rest of the world's.

4. *This teaching applies equally to men and women.* This is not a special teaching just for women, or just for men. If you commit yourself to your spouse until one of you dies, then the chances are much greater that your marriage will last. The very nature of your commitment will make it last because you will know there are no easy ways out.

A friend of mine who has been married for fifteen years was told that she and her husband must be unusually compatible to have been married for so long. Her response was, "I'm sorry, but I resent that. We've had to put a lot of effort into making this marriage work." That's exactly what you'll do if you know there's no way out. I believe most people would not divorce their mates if they felt they couldn't remarry.

God wants us to be "one-spouse people." He allows us to divorce and remarry, but we will pay a terrible price in our spirits (see Malachi 2:15-17).

The Perfect Match?

Mr. and Mrs. Mateus Minas, of Evora, Portugal, were both born on January 1, 1801. They lived through an entire century, then died on December 31, 1900, within hours of each other.

Mr. and Mrs. Jonath Graber of Freeman, South Dakota, celebrated their 50th wedding anniversary with every member of the original wedding party present.

Notable Quotables

"A happy marriage is a long conversation that always seems too short."
—Andre Maurois

"The true index of a man's character is the health of his wife."
—Cyril Connolly

"An ideal of love: To love with all desire and yet to be as kind as an old man past desire."
—W. B. Yeats

Bon Voyage!

You are coming to the end of this Campus Magazine. Perhaps you're anxious to get started on your own Spirit-filled adventure in love. Here are some reminders to help you start out right.

First, make certain that you are marrying a Christian. This is extremely important. I can't emphasize this enough. Don't marry a non-Christian (2 Corinthians 6:14; 1 Corinthians 7:39). If you do, you're headed for nothing but trouble.

Remember, a Christian is not just one who goes to church or reads the Bible or believes Christian principles. A Christian, according to Romans 8:9-10, is one in whom the Spirit of Christ dwells. If Jesus is living in and working through your spouse-to-be, he is a believer. If Jesus isn't present, it doesn't matter how nice she is, or how many good works he does, or how often she goes to church.

Second, make sure you're out of Fantasyland before you get married. This is difficult because most of us are willfully self-deceived about our spouses-to-be. We don't want them to have any weaknesses, so our minds conveniently camouflage the obvious signs. But the key to surviving the aftermath of your honeymoon is to open your eyes before you get married.

Plan activities together that put the two of you in challenging situations. Go on a hiking trip, or retreat, or work on a demanding project together. See how you handle stress, and other problems, as a couple. It is better to find out now what your spouse-to-be is really like rather than to find out the hard way after you are married.

Third, marry someone who wants to

grow spiritually. You want someone who will be constantly moving ahead in his relationship with the Lord. You want someone who will stimulate you to greater growth. If you don't have this, you have the wrong person.

Fourth, make certain that God wants the two of you to get married. Just because you both are Christians doesn't mean that God wants you to be married. Never mind how you feel about your loved one for a moment; can you say without a shadow of doubt that God wants you together? If you don't have his perfect peace, back off until you get it (review "Knowing God's Peace" in chapter 5).

Fifth, make certain that both of you are committing yourselves to a lifetime marriage relationship. You want to enter into a marriage covenant relationship, not just a marriage contract.

When you get married, the state you live in issues you a marriage license, which is a legal and binding contract subject to the laws of that state. You have to have this in order to be married in the eyes of the state. However, your marriage should be more than a contractual relationship; it should also be a covenant relationship.

Contracts generally are entered into for protection. The two parties write down what they propose to do so that if one of the parties reneges his part of the deal, the other can legally get compensation.

In a covenant, both parties are saying, "I promise I will do the following—whether or not you hold up your end of the agreement." A covenant is based upon your honesty and integrity, *not* upon the integrity of the party you are covenanting with. If you enter into this type of commitment, the chances are good that your marriage will be happy and last a lifetime.